Sea Fishing from Shore and Boat

By
Various Authors

A Short History of Fishing

Fishing, in its broadest sense – is the activity of catching fish. It is an ancient practice dating back at least 40,000 years. Since the sixteenth century fishing vessels have been able to cross oceans in pursuit of fish and since the nineteenth century it has been possible to use larger vessels and in some cases process the fish on board. Techniques for catching fish include varied methods such as hand gathering, spearing, netting, angling and trapping.

Isotopic analysis of the skeletal remains of **Tianyuan man**, a 40,000 year old modern human from eastern Asia, has shown that he regularly consumed freshwater fish. As well as this, archaeological features such as shell middens, discarded fish-bones and cave paintings show that sea foods were important for early man's survival and were consumed in significant quantities. The first civilisation to practice organised fishing was the Egyptians however, as the River Nile was so full of fish. The **Egyptians** invented various implements and methods for fishing and these are clearly illustrated in tomb scenes, drawings and papyrus documents. Simple **reed boats** served for fishing. Woven nets, weir baskets made from willow branches, harpoons and hook and line (the hooks having a length of between eight millimetres and eighteen centimetres) were all being used. By the **twelfth dynasty**, metal hooks with barbs were also utilised.

Despite the Egyptian's strong history of fishing, later Greek cultures rarely depicted the trade, due to its perceived low social status. There is a wine cup however, dating from c.500 BC, that shows a boy crouched on a rock with a fishing-rod in his right hand and a basket in his left. In the water below there is a rounded object of the same material with an opening on the top. This has been identified as a fish-cage used for keeping live fish, or as a fish-trap. One of the other major Grecian sources on fishing is Oppian of Corycus, who wrote a major treatise on sea fishing, the *Halieulica* or *Halieutika*, composed between 177 and 180. This is the earliest such work to have survived intact to the modern day. Oppian describes various means of fishing including the use of nets cast from boats, scoop nets held open by a hoop, spears and tridents, and various traps 'which work while their masters sleep.' Oppian's description of fishing with a 'motionless' net is also very interesting:

> *The fishers set up very light nets of buoyant flax and wheel in a circle round about while they violently strike the surface of the sea with their oars and make a din with sweeping blow of poles. At the*

flashing of the swift oars and the noise the fish bound in terror and rush into the bosom of the net which stands at rest, thinking it to be a shelter: foolish fishes which, frightened by a noise, enter the gates of doom. Then the fishers on either side hasten with the ropes to draw the net ashore...

The earliest English essay on recreational fishing was published in 1496, shortly after the invention of the printing press! Unusually for the time, its author was a woman; Dame Juliana Berners, the prioress of the Benedictine Sopwell Nunnery (Hertforshire). The essay was titled *Treatyse of Fysshynge with an Angle* and was published in a larger book, forming part of a treatise on hawking, hunting and heraldry. These were major interests of the nobility, and the publisher, Wynkyn der Worde was concerned that the book should be kept from those who were not gentlemen, since their immoderation in angling might 'utterly destroye it.' The roots of recreational fishing itself go much further back however, and the earliest evidence of the fishing reel comes from a fourth century AD work entitled *Lives of Famous Mortals*.

Many credit the first recorded use of an artificial fly (fly fishing) to an even earlier source - to the Roman Claudius Aelianus near the end of the second century.

He described the practice of Macedonian anglers on the Astraeus River, '...they have planned a snare for the fish, and get the better of them by their fisherman's craft. . . . They fasten red wool round a hook, and fit on to the wool two feathers which grow under a cock's wattles, and which in colour are like wax.' Recreational fishing for sport or leisure only really took off during the sixteenth and seventeenth centuries though, and coincides with the publication of Izaak Walton's *The Compleat Angler* in 1653. This is seen as the definitive work that champions the position of the angler who loves fishing for the sake of fishing itself. More than 300 editions have since been published, demonstrating its unstoppable popularity.

Big-game fishing only started as a sport after the invention of the motorised boat. In 1898, Dr. Charles Frederick Holder, a marine biologist and early conservationist, virtually invented this sport and went on to publish many articles and books on the subject. His works were especially noted for their combination of accurate scientific detail with exciting narratives. Big-game fishing is also a recreational pastime, though requires a largely purpose built boat for the hunting of large fish such as the billfish (swordfish, marlin and sailfish), larger tunas (bluefin, yellowfin and bigeye), and sharks (mako, great white, tiger and hammerhead). Such developments have only really gained prominence in the twentieth century. The motorised boat has also meant that commercial fishing, as well as fish farming has emerged on a massive scale. Large trawling ships are common and one of the strongest markets in the world is the cod trade which fishes roughly 23,000 tons from the Northwest Atlantic, 475,000 tons from the Northeast Atlantic and 260,000 tons from the Pacific.

These truly staggering amounts show just how much fishing has changed; from its early hunter-gatherer beginnings, to a small and specialised trade in Egyptian and Grecian societies, to a gentleman's pastime in fifteenth century England right up to the present day. We hope that the reader enjoys this book, and is inspired by fishing's long and intriguing past to find out more about this truly fascinating subject. Enjoy.

FISHING

To y^e R. noble Christopher Duke of Albemarle, Earle of Torington, Baron Monke of Potheridge, Beauchamp and Teys, K. of y^e Garter, Captaine of his Ma.ties life Guard, L. Leutenant of Essex and Devonshire, one of the Gentlemen of his Ma.ties Bedchamber, and one of the Lord of his most Honourable Privy Councell &c. This Place of Fishing is most humbly Dedicated by Ric Blome.

CONTENTS

LIST OF ILLUSTRATIONS

FISHING

LIST OF ILLUSTRATIONS

CHAPTER XXIV

BRITISH SEA FISH

By G. A. BOULENGER, F.R.S., V.P.Z.S., &c.

THE GREY MULLETS (*Mugil*)

THE fishes of this genus are easily recognised by their feebly compressed body and short, rounded head, both covered with large, strongly overlapping scales; the infero-lateral eyes, better visible from below than from above; the absence of a lateral line; the small transverse mouth, furnished with small or setiform teeth; the presence of two dorsal fins, the first formed of 4 or 5 spinous rays, the second, opposed to the anal, formed of a few branched rays; the shortness of the pectoral fin, which is inserted rather high up the side, and the position of the ventral fins about midway between the bases of the pectoral and first dorsal fins. These ventral fins are neither free from the pectoral girdle, as in *Belone* and salmon, pike, and carp, nor attached to the clavicles, as in perches; the bones on which they are inserted are suspended from a pair of long, rod-like bones, the so-called post-clavicles, which descend from the shoulder. In other respects, too, it may be said that the *Mugilidæ*, now placed among the *Persesoces*, hold an intermediate position between the soft-rayed and the spiny-rayed fishes, as we have mentioned above à *propos* of the gar-fish.

The branchial apparatus of these fishes is peculiar for the presence of series of long, closely-set appendages or gill-rakers on the concave side of each gill-arch, these gill-rakers curved inwards and meeting similar appendages inserted on the mucous membrane of the pharynx, to form a sort of filtering apparatus by which the thicker matter engulfed by the fish is retained in the mouth, whilst the water is expelled through the gill openings; for the *Mullus* feed to a great extent on diatoms in mud and on decayed animal and vegetable substances. In consequence of this régime the gut is extremely elongate, coiled up in numerous convolutions. But they also consume great quantities of bivalve and univalve mollusca, to crush the shells of which the stomach is provided with a thick-walled muscular appendage much like the gizzard of a bird.

51.—GREY MULLET.

52.—*RED MULLET.*

Most of the grey mullets are sea fishes, but resorting in preference to estuaries and marshy ponds, where they spawn, and also ascending rivers beyond tidal influence. They are sometimes kept, and breed in fresh-water ponds. All are remarkable for their agility and their habit of constantly leaping over the surface of the water.

The genus *Mullus* is of almost world-wide distribution. About eighty species are known, three of which occur in the British islands :—

1. The thick-lipped grey mullet (*Mugil chelo*).
2. The golden grey mullet (*M. auratus*).
3. The thin-lipped grey mullet (*M. capito*).

As these species are often confounded, and as much remains to be done in ascertaining their exact distribution on our coasts, it is necessary to enter somewhat fully into their distinctive characters.

The first species, *M. chelo*, which appears to be the commonest, is remarkable for its thick upper lip, often beset with large wart-like papillæ on its inferior half; the diameter of the upper lip, in the middle, in the adult is more than half that of the eye ; the chin is entirely covered by the bones of the lower jaw, or they leave between them only a very narrow strip uncovered. The pectoral fin measures at least three-fourths the length of the head, and there is no free scale above its axil.

M. auratus is intermediate between the preceding and the following species. The upper lip is thin, its diameter not more than half that of the eye, and hardly projects beyond the cleft of the mouth, which is nearly terminal ; the rami of the lower jaw leave a lanceolate space on the chin uncovered. The pectoral fin measures at least three-fourths of the length of the head, and there is no free scale above its axil.

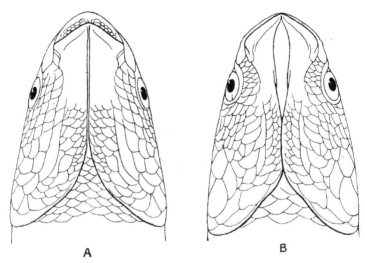

LOWER VIEW OF HEAD OF (A) *Mugil chelo;* (B) *M. capito.*

In *M. capito* the upper lip is even thinner than in *M. auratus*, its width always much less than half the diameter of the eye ; there is a lanceolate naked space on the chin as in *M. auratus.* The pectoral fin is shorter than in either of the preceding species, and a free scale is present above its axil.

The three species are similarly coloured, grey, or greyish brown, above, silvery white below, with more or less distinct dark streaks following the series of scales. But *M. auratus* is distinguished by the presence of a golden spot on the gill-cover, whence the name, "golden grey mullet."

The thick-lipped grey mullet reaches a length of three feet, and is, according to Mr. J. T. Cunningham, the only species commonly found at Plymouth; it is also the one most frequently sold on the London market. The two other species do not exceed a length of two feet. *M. capito* is on record from Scotland, the south coast of England, and Ireland; it has a very extensive distribution, occurring from the coasts of Scandinavia all along the Atlantic to the Cape of Good Hope, being also found in the Mediterranean and the Lower Nile.

M. auratus, which has nearly the same distribution, but is not known to occur south of the mouth of the Congo, where it is common, is sometimes sold in the London market, and specimens from Cheltenham are preserved in the British Museum, from the collection of the late Mr. Francis Day, who confounded this species with *M. capito* in his work on British fishes.

It is much to be desired that anglers should pay due attention to the distinctive marks of these three kinds of grey mullet, in order to throw more light on their distribution on our coasts.

THE COD FAMILY (*Gadidæ*)

The relations and systematic position of this group of fishes, so important from an economic point of view, have been, and are still, a subject of contention among ichthyologists. Having no spines to their fins, the Gadids used, in Cuvierian days, to be associated with the herrings, Salmonids, pike, and such like, in the artificially conceived order of Malacopterygians or soft-finned fishes. But, on the ground of their air - bladder being closed, or deprived of a pneumatic duct communicating with the digestive canal, such as is characteristic of the true Malacopterygians and of most other "soft-finned" fishes, they were removed from them and placed with the flat fishes, or Pleuronectids, in a sub-order, "*Anacanthini*," regarded as intermediate in position between the Acanthopterygians, or spiny-finned fishes, and the Malacopterygians. It has, however, been shown, I should even say conclusively proved, that the flat fishes bear no relationship to the Gadids ; they are, in the opinion of the writer, most nearly akin to the John Dories, or Zeidæ, with which they are connected by an extinct type, *Amphistium*, from the Eocene, giving us an idea of what the common ancestor of these forms, so different in appearance at the present day, must have been like. Although we have no hesitation in removing the Gadids from the vicinity of the flat fishes or of the Malacopterygians, we find it difficult to suggest which group the Anacanthini, now restricted to the Gadidæ and the Macruridæ, may have been derived from ; in trying to reconstitute the phylogeny of the bony fishes, we should probably seek for their direct ancestors among the sub-order Haplomi, including the pike

and the numerous allies of the Bombay duck
(*Harpodon*), the Scopelidæ, rather than from any
of the Acanthopterygians, as was at one time
believed.

Any of our readers who might feel interested in
the recent views on the relationships of the Gadidæ,
should refer to the paper by the writer in the *Annals
and Magazine of Natural History*, vol. x. 1902, p. 295,
and to another by Mr. C. Tate Regan in the same
journal, vol. xi. 1903, p. 459.

The Gadidæ may be described as Teleosts with
closed air-bladder, with all the fin-rays articulated,
made up of distinct segments, and flexible, with a
perfectly symmetrical caudal fin which is not supported by an enlarged fan-shaped bone, and with
the ventral fins inserted in advance of the pectoral
fins, and not connected with the bones of the
shoulder-girdle otherwise than by ligament. The
scales are small, smooth, and thin, and the chin is
frequently provided with a fleshy appendage or
barbel. The very forward position of the ventral
fins serves to distinguish these fishes from all other
piscine members of our fauna in which the body is
symmetrical and the fin-rays are all articulated and
flexible.

About 120 species are distinguished, mostly
marine, many being adapted to life at great depths;
all are carnivorous. They inhabit chiefly the
northern seas, but many abyssal forms occur
between the Tropics and in the southern parts of
the Atlantic and Pacific. They are represented in

our waters by eight genera, which may be distinguished in the following manner :—

I. Caudal fin truncated or notched.

1. *Gadus.* Three dorsal and two anal fins.

2. *Merluccius,* hake. Two dorsal fins, the front one short, the hind one long ; a single, long anal fin.

II. Caudal fin rounded.

A. Two dorsal fins, the front one short but well developed, the hind one long ; a single, long anal fin.

3. *Molva,* ling. Ventral fins with several rays ; dorsal and anal not quite reaching the caudal ; enlarged teeth in the lower jaw.

4. *Lota,* burbot. Ventral fins with several rays ; dorsal and anal fins reaching the caudal ; teeth all small.

5. *Phycis,* fork-beard. Ventral fin reduced to a bifid filament.

B. Two dorsal fins, the front one rudimentary ; a single, long anal fin.

6. *Raniceps,* tadpole fish. No nasal barbels.

7. *Onus (Motella),* rocklings. Nasal barbels.

C. A single dorsal and a single anal fin, both very long.

8. *Brosmius,* tusk or torsk.

The burbot is our only fresh-water representative of the Gadidæ.

Only the first genus, of which the cod is the type, need occupy us here as containing two fishes, the coal-fish and the pollack, which afford sport to anglers. It is represented on our coasts by eight species, some of which are sufficiently nearly allied to offer some difficulties in their determination. These difficulties will, we think, disappear if use be made of the following synopsis or key which we have drawn up for their easy identification.

I. Base of first anal fin not or but slightly longer than that of the second dorsal fin; upper jaw projecting more or less beyond the lower.

1. *G. morrhua*, cod. Mental barbel at least half as long as the eye; first anal fin with 17 to 20 rays; lateral line whitish.

2. *G. æglefinus*, haddock. Mental barbel very short; first anal fin with 22 to 25 rays; lateral line dark.

3. *G. minutus*, power or poor cod. Mental barbel as long as or a little shorter than the eye; anal fin with 25 to 29 rays.

II. Base of first anal fin considerably longer than that of the second dorsal.

A. Upper jaw projecting a little beyond the lower; a dark spot at the root of the pectoral fin.

4. *G. merlangus*, whiting. No barbel; no dark bars.

5. *G. luscus*, bib or pout. A mental barbel, nearly as long as the eye; body deep, with more or less distinct dark bars.

B. Lower jaw projecting more or less beyond the upper; usually a dark spot in the axil of the pectoral fin.

6. *G. virens*, coal-fish. A small mental barbel, sometimes rudimentary; vent below the posterior half of the first dorsal fin.

7. *G. pollachius*, pollack. No barbel; lower jaw strongly projecting; vent below the anterior half of the first dorsal fin.

8. *G. poutassou*, poutassou. No barbel; second dorsal fin not longer than the first; vent before the vertical of the first dorsal fin.

THE COAL-FISH (*Gadus virens*). — Also called green cod, black pollack, saith, and sillock. The three dorsal fins are low, the second the longest at the base, but shorter than the first anal fin. The lower jaw projects a little beyond the upper in the adult, scarcely at all in the very young, and is provided with a very small mental barbel, which may be so reduced as to be easily overlooked. The vent is situated vertically below the posterior half of the first dorsal fin. The upper parts vary from dark grey or olive to blackish, shading off into silvery white towards the belly; the lateral line is whitish; usually a dark spot in the axil of the pectoral fin, not visible when the fin is folded. Old specimens are darker than the young.

This fish grows to a large size; specimens a little over $3\frac{1}{2}$ feet are on record, but the usual length is between 2 and 3 feet.

The range of the coal-fish is a very wide one, and nearly coincides with that of the cod, although of a somewhat more southern character, as it extends to both east and west coasts of the North Atlantic,

and it is occasionally found in the Mediterranean.
It is especially common in the north, though rarely
entering the Baltic; it becomes rare south of the
English Channel. Its limits of distribution appear
to be between 46° and 80° lat. in the Western
Atlantic, between 40° and 70° in the Eastern
Atlantic. It descends to a depth of 70 fathoms.
The breeding season with us is said to begin in
January, and to continue through February, March,
and April; according to Brook, the spawning on
the coast of Scotland may even begin in December.
On the coast of Massachusetts the spawning period
has been ascertained to be in November and December. Unlike the cod and the haddock, the coal-fish
is, to a great extent, a surface-swimming fish, con-
gregating together in large schools, and moving
from place to place in search of food ; large specimens, however, prefer deep water, and rarely fall
a prey to the sportsman.

THE POLLACK (*Gadus pollachius*). — This fish,
which grows to a length of three feet, is recog-
nisable among the species with the base of the
anal fin considerably longer than that of the second
dorsal, by its very prominent lower jaw, the chin,
which is deprived of a barbel, extending forward a
good deal beyond the end of the snout, and by the
position of the vent, which, owing to the somewhat
longer first anal fin, is situated vertically below the
anterior half of the first dorsal fin, instead of being
below its posterior half, as in the coal-fish. The eye

is also larger in proportion than in the latter species. The colour is brown or olive above, the lateral line darker, yellowish, or golden below, often with a dark spot superiorly in the axil of the pectoral fin. The pollack, or lythe, occurs on the coasts of Europe, as far south as the western parts of the Mediterranean. It is extremely common on our rocky coasts. It is, for a considerable period of its existence, a surface fish, and is usually found not far from land, chasing schools of young cod and herrings; but full-grown examples frequent the deeper waters offshore. The breeding season, on the British coasts, lasts from December till May, taking place earlier in the north than in the south.

A very full account of the external and osteological characters of the coal-fish and pollack, compared with the cod, will be found in a paper by Dr. H. C. Williamson, published in Part III. of the Twentieth Annual Report of the Fishery Board for Scotland, 1902, pp. 228–287, pls. iv.–xi.

The Sea-Bass and Sea-Perch (*Serranidæ*)

This family, one of the largest of the class Pisces, and formed almost exclusively of marine species, is very nearly related to the true perches; the characters on which they have been separated from them are mainly osteological and need not be explained in a work of this kind. Suffice it to say that the eyeball is supported, in the *Serranidæ*, by a bony process of the second suborbital bone, called

a subocular shelf, of which there is no trace in the
true perches, a character which can be readily ascertained on any specimen, even without dissection,
when once understood. The black bass of the
fresh-waters of America noticed above, which bear
no special affinity to our sea-bass, are more nearly
related to the fresh-water perches, and, like them,
lack the subocular shelf.

The Serranidæ are typical Acanthopterygians with
the air-bladder, when present, as is usually the case,
closed, with the anterior portion of the dorsal
fin formed of pungent spines, and with the ventral
fins inserted below the pectorals and composed
of 1 spine and 5 soft, branched rays. Some of
the bones of the head, as the preorbital and the
elements of the gill-cover, are also frequently ser-
rate or armed with more or less strong spines.

In the sea-bass of our coasts and estuaries (*Morone
labrax*, often called *Labrax lupus*), the dorsal fin is
divided into two distinct parts, the anterior formed
of 8 to 10 spines, the posterior of 1 spine and
12 soft rays; the anal fin, which is opposed to the
second dorsal, is formed of 3 spines and 10 to
12 soft rays. The body is elongate and compressed, covered with rather small, rough scales,
there being 65 to 80 in the lateral line; the mouth
is large and cleft to below the eye; the præopercle,
or bone limiting the cheek towards the gill-cover,
is serrated, the serræ on its lower border being
larger, more widely set, and directed forwards; the
gill-cover is armed with strong spines. The colour

is silvery, more grey on the back, the young sometimes with scattered blackish dots ; a dark spot on
the gill-cover.   The sea-bass often attains a length
of 3 feet and a weight of 10 lbs.   Yarrell alludes
to a specimen weighing 28 lbs.

Morone labrax, the sea-wolf of the Greeks, a voracious and cunning fish, of excellent quality, and
much prized in France, where it is known as "Bars"
and "Loup," inhabits the coasts of Europe, from
Norway to the Mediterranean.   It is rare in Scotland north of the Firth of Forth, and is not recorded from the Orkneys and Shetland.   But it is
common in the English Channel and on the south
coast of Ireland.   According to Couch and Day,
the breeding takes place in summer on our southern
coast, but Raffaele found the ripe ova in the Mediterranean from January to the beginning of March.

The sea-bass is represented on the east coast of
America by a close ally, the striped bass, or rock-
fish (*Morone lineata*), which grows to a length of
6 feet, and is one of the most important game
fishes of America.   It is abundant in the estuaries
of great rivers from the St. Lawrence to North
Carolina, but becomes rather rare farther south and
in the Gulf of Mexico.   Unlike its European relative, it is strictly an anadromous fish, living chiefly
in salt or brackish water, and entering fresh water
to spawn.

We have stated above that the Serranidæ are
almost exclusively marine.   Among the few exceptions to the rule are two other near allies of the

BRITISH SEA FISH 225

sea-bass, the white bass (*Morone multilineata*) and the yellow bass (*M. interrupta*), excellent game and food fishes of the great lakes and rivers of North America; they grow to about 18 inches. The sea-perches are represented on our southwest coast by three species: *Serranus cabrilla*, *Polyprion americanus*, and *Epinephelus æneus*. These fishes are of no importance to the angler, but as it is not generally known that some members of this family are normally hermaphrodite, it may be interesting to point out that the first of the above-named presents this condition, each of the two genital glands being divided into a testicular and an ovarian portion, which ripen simultaneously, thus rendering auto-fecundation perfectly possible.

Anglers in Florida are familiar with several species of the genus *Epinephelus*, known as groupers and jew-fish, many being remarkable for their vivid colours or huge size. The spinous and the soft portions of the dorsal fin are continuous instead of being separated by a notch or short interspace as in the perch and sea-bass, and some of the teeth in the jaws are hinged at the base and depressible. Most of them are excellent for food, the better kinds being sold at from twelve to fifteen cents a pound. The red grouper (*E. morio*) is the most abundant and best-known species of the genus: it is olive-grey or pale brown, with darker brown marblings, with the lower part of the head and breast usually red or salmon-colour, the inside of the mouth posteriorly bright orange; it reaches a length of 2 or 3 feet, and a weight of 20 to 40 lbs. The black grouper (*E. nigritus*), varying from chocolate-brown to blackish grey, and without markings or with faint blotches, is an immense fish, reaching a length of 6 feet and a weight of 500 lbs. Another giant of the Florida coast is the spotted jew-fish (*E. itaiara*) of about the same size as the black grouper, and remarkable for its very broad, depressed head ; although called "spotted," the adults are nearly uniform brown, the spots or bands, which are distinct in the young, disappearing with age.

Another monster fish, which gives great sport to the angler, is the Californian jew-fish, or black sea-bass, *Stereolepis gigas*. It resembles the Florida jew-fish in shape, but differs in having the spinous dorsal fin distinct from the soft. At Avalon, in Southern California, where the American Tuna Club has its headquarters—the club consisting of some 300 members of any nationality—the tuna fishing lasts only from May to the end of September, after which time the black sea-bass is the chief objective of the sportsman, the aim being to catch these immense fish with as light a tackle as possible. *Stereolepis* attains a length of 7 feet and a weight of 500 lbs. Professor C. F. Holder, who has paid special attention to the habits of this fish, says : " It is a bottom feeder, and is fished for on the edge of the kelp in 30 or 40 feet of water. The strike comes as a nibble, but when hooked the fish is away with a rush that has been known to demoralise experienced anglers. I have seen a 200 - lb. fish

53.—*BASS.*

54.— JEW FISH—FLORIDA.

snap the largest shark-line like a thread, and large specimens straighten out an iron shark-hook; yet the skilled wielders of the rod catch these giants of the tribe with a line that is not larger than some eyeglass cords."

Similar giant sea-perches occur on the coasts of South America, of India, of Japan, and of New South Wales. The sheepshead and sea bream (*Sparidæ*), and the drummers, squeteagues, and croakers (*Sciænidæ*), representatives of families nearly related to the *Serranidæ*, are some of the fishes most familiar to the angler in Florida waters.

THE MACKEREL FAMILY (*Scombriaæ*)

Acanthopterygians with non-protractile, beak-like upper jaw; fusiform body, without or with very small, smooth scales; a spinous dorsal fin of slender spines, folding into a sheath, and longer soft dorsal and anal fins broken up into finlets; the pectoral fin pointed or falciform and inserted high up the side, and the caudal bifid or crescentic, formed of numerous rays deeply forked at the base and embracing the bone on which they are inserted. This family embraces about 50 species, represented in the seas of nearly the whole world. The mackerels and tunnies are its best-known representatives, the former coast fishes, the latter ranging through the open seas.

THE MACKEREL (*Scomber · scombrus*) is too familiar a fish to require description, but as a second species of the same genus is sometimes found on our coasts, it is well to indicate its sure recognition-marks, viz., 11 to 15 (exceptionally 10 or 16) slender spines in the first dorsal fin (on the anterior part of the back, folding into a sheath), the diameter of the eye $\frac{1}{5}$ to $\frac{1}{6}$ the length of the head, and the absence of a swim-bladder. The waving or vermicular bluish black bands which adorn the back of the mackerel are not a constant specific character; some individuals have straight transverse stripes on the back, others are closely spotted (*S. punctatus*), while others still have been described as "scribbled" (*S. scriptus*). Looked upon by some authors as distinct species, these aberrant forms are now generally regarded as variations of the common mackerel, with which they occur promiscuously.[1] I have also seen specimens which are uniform dark steel-blue above, without any markings, and Professor Collett remarks of Norwegian specimens that the colour of the back may sometimes be an unvaried black. The usual length of the mackerel is between 12 and 16 inches, but specimens 2 feet long are on record.

The mackerel is an inhabitant of the North Atlantic, being found on both its coasts, at some places and at certain seasons in extraordinary abundance. The limits of its range may be drawn between latitudes 36° and 71° in the Eastern Atlantic, between

---

[1] The structural and colour variations of the mackerel have formed the subject of two important recent papers by W. Garstang, *Journ. Mar. Biol. Ass.* (2), v. 1898, p. 235; and by H. C. Williamson, *Ann. Rep. Fisher. Board, Scotland*, xviii., pt. iii., 1900, p. 294.

55.—SCAD OR HORSE MACKEREL.

56.—THE COMMON MACKEREL.

35° and 56° in the Western Atlantic. The question of the migrations of this fish has been much discussed, and various extraordinary theories propounded to account for its movements. The general consensus is at present to regard the mackerel as a shore-loving fish, restricted to comparatively small distances in its wanderings, which appear to be regulated by the temperature of the ocean. As in other fishes moving in shoals, the sardine, for example, the irregular appearances of the mackerel cause a great disturbance in an important industry; on certain coasts the movements of the fish are quite uncertain, sometimes in one direction and sometimes in another, or the fish may disappear almost entirely for several years, subsequently reappearing after a lengthy absence. As observed by Brown Goode, who has paid special attention to this subject, it is not certain, of course, that this disappearance indicates an entire absence of the fish from the locality, but the fish may for some reason remain in the depth of the sea, or some change in the character of the animal life in it, which constitutes the food of the fish, may cause them to shift their quarters.

As regards the movements on our coasts,[1] these commence towards the end of winter, and by May and June large shoals of breeding fishes are to be found close inland. On the east coast of Britain,

[1] *Cf.* E. J. Allen, " Report on the Present State of Knowledge with regard to the Habits and Migrations of the Mackerel," *Journ. Mar. Biol. Ass.* (2), v. 1897, p. 1.

according to J. T. Cunningham, very few mackerel
are taken north of Norfolk, whilst on the west coast
of Scotland they are more plentiful. On the west
coast of England they are taken regularly in summer
in some abundance ; at the Isle of Man the fishing
lasts from May to September. In Ireland the prin-
cipal mackerel fishing is in the south-west, but they
are taken in summer all along the west coast.

Mr. Cunningham has thus lately summarised
what has been ascertained as to the migrations of
the mackerel on the English coast :—" At Plymouth there is no month in the year in which
mackerel are not taken, but they are scarcest in
December and January. This is presumably the
time when the fish are farthest from the coast,
feeding in the more distant water where the temperature is higher. The few caught in those months
in 1889–90 were taken fifteen to forty miles south
of Plymouth. In February they become more abundant, the largest catches being 4000 to 5000, the
fish still a long way off, twenty to thirty miles from
Start Point. In March and April the fish are still
a long way off, at least thirty miles from the Sound
in March, twenty miles in April. In May, however,
the fish approach the land while spawning, being
taken at the end of the month only a mile or so
outside the breakwater. In June they remain inshore, but these are the smaller fish, and much
larger fish are caught off Ushant and the Scilly
Islands. At this time fishing by hooks commences.
In July and August mackerel enter Plymouth Sound,

where they are taken by whiffing lines, and in good years by seine. After the beginning of September they leave the Sound, and are caught a few miles south of the Eddystone. In October and November they are caught from four miles south of the Eddystone to twenty or thirty miles south of Start Point. Off the coasts of Norfolk and Suffolk there is a valuable drift-net fishery for mackerel, which is carried on in May and June, and also from the 1st September to the middle of November. I do not know why they should be absent in July and August. It seems probable, however, that these fish only visit this part of the North Sea in summer, that they spawn there in May and June, and that they retire to the Channel in the latter part of November."

The mackerel is a pelagic - feeding fish, not a ground-feeder, like the cod, for instance ; its food consists chiefly of small fish, spawn, and minute crustacea—free-swimming organisms.

A second species, the Spanish mackerel or coly (*S. colias*, also called *S. pneumatophorus*), distinguished by the smaller number of spines (7 to 10) in the anterior dorsal fin, the larger eye (more than a quarter the length of the head), and the presence of a swim-bladder, appears irregularly on our coasts, although on the south coast of Cornwall, according to Couch, three or four hundred are occasionally seen at a time. The distribution of the Spanish mackerel is a much more extensive one even than that of the common species, as it occurs over the greater part of the Atlantic, from Great Britain and the extreme north of the United States to Brazil and the Cape of Good Hope, where it is very plentiful, as well as in the Pacific Ocean, whence it is on record from California, the Galapagos Islands, China, and Japan. Although of importance as a food-fish, the Spanish mackerel cannot compare with its more northern relative, its flesh being softer and decomposing more rapidly. Americans call this fish the chub, or thimble-eyed mackerel, the name Spanish mackerel being applied by them to another Scombrid, *Scombromorus maculatus.*

THE TUNNY (*Thunnus thynnus*).—Tunnies and bonitoes are closely related to the mackerels, differing in the presence of enlarged scales on the pectoral region, forming a corselet, and of a longitudinal keel on each side of the caudal peduncle. They live chiefly in the open ocean, wandering in large schools, preying upon other pelagic fish, and approaching land only when attracted by the abundance of some special food. Most of the species have consequently a very extensive distribution, and the true tunny is almost cosmopolitan, although of rare occurrence in the north or at corresponding latitudes in the southern hemisphere. They are among the most beautiful and powerful of fishes, and admirably adapted to rapid motion. In connection with their extremely active life, allusion should be made to the fact, first ascertained by John Davy in 1839, that the temperature of the blood of a tunny may be considerably

higher than that of the surrounding water, a dis-
covery which disposed of the time-honoured division
of vertebrate animals into warm-blooded and cold-
blooded.

The Tunny, which is of such enormous commercial importance in Spain and Portugal and on
the south and west coasts of France, and reaches a
length of 9 or 10 feet, has 13 or 14 spines in the
anterior dorsal fin, 7 to 9 finlets above and as many
below the tail, and the pectoral fin not longer,
usually shorter, than the head. Its appearances on
our coasts are very irregular, and never in great
numbers, but it is regularly fished for off the northwest coast of Brittany.

Although of no great reputation as a game-fish
in the Atlantic, the tunny is much sought for by
anglers on the coast of Southern California. Professor Holder, whom we have quoted above *à propos*
of the black sea-bass, says : " The most sensational
fish of these waters is the leaping tuna, which well
compares with the tarpon, and personally I prefer
it to its Florida and Texas rival, and in my experience the average large tuna is a match for two
tarpons of the same size. The tuna is the tiger
of the Californian seas, a living meteor which strikes
like a whirlwind, and when played with a rod that
is not a billiard cue or a club in stiffness, will give
the average man the contest of his life."

A second species of tunny is known as the Alba-
core, or Germon (*T. alalonga*), distinguished from the
preceding by the longer, sickle-shaped pectoral fin,

which, in the adult, measures nearly one-third or two-fifths of the total length. Its distribution is nearly as extensive as that of the typical species, but as a food-fish it is of much less value, the flesh being coarse and oily, and it only grows to about three feet. It is common in the south of Europe, but only a few stragglers have occurred on our coasts as far north as the Orkneys. Large quantities are captured in the southern parts of the Bay of Biscay in July and August.

Both species of tunny are the object of important fisheries on the coast of Portugal, and their variations and movements have been studied with special care by the King of Portugal, who has published a large illustrated memoir, entitled "A Pesca do Atum no Algarve im 1898, por Don Carlos de Bragança" (Lisbon, 1899), with a French résumé. The excellent figures and the charts accompanying this memoir should prove of great utility to tuna fishers.

Other less important Scombrids of exceptional occurrence on our coasts are the bonito (*Euthynnus pelamys*), the pelamid (*Sarda mediterranea*), and the plain bonito (*Auxis rochei*).

THE SHARKS (*Carchariidæ*)

The class fishes is divided primarily into three sub-classes : Teleostomes (the bony fishes and sturgeons), Chondropterygians (sharks, rays, chimæras), and Cyclostomes (lampreys and hag-fish). All the fishes previously dealt with in this work are Teleostomes, and of the division Teleosteans, which embrace the great majority of living fishes. We have now a few words to say about a very different type belonging to the second sub-class, as two forms of it, the blue shark and porbeagle, are of interest to the angler on our coasts.

Sharks, in a wide sense, may be defined as having the skeleton entirely cartilaginous or merely calcified, without bone, with the integument devoid of scales, but studded with shagreen denticles, the structure of which corresponds with that of teeth; these denticles being sometimes identical, but for size, with the teeth with which the mouth is beset; with several (5 to 7) gill-openings on each side, which are exposed or covered with frill-like folds, but always devoid of opercles, and in which the males are provided with "claspers," copulatory organs developed at the hinder margin of the ventral fins. Sharks, and their near relatives the skates, which are only much-flattened sharks with the gill-openings on the lower surface instead of on the sides, are very "old" fishes, which can be traced back to Palæozoic times. Although primitive, or generalised, in structure, they are in many respects more highly organised than the more modern Teleostean fishes, and the great size to which some of them attain makes them objects of general interest.

Many species of sharks and dog-fish occur on our coasts, either as regular or accidental visitors. Among the latter, the largest is the basking shark (*Selacha maxima*), of which a male specimen 28 feet long, obtained near Shanklin, Isle of Wight, in 1876, is exhibited in the Natural History Museum at South Kensington.

The blue shark (*Carcharias glaucus*) only grows to 11 or 12 feet. It is found irregularly on all our coasts, whilst in Cornwall it is said to be abundant during the latter part of the summer and early in the autumn; it is not rare on the south coast of Ireland, where it is said to do great mischief to nets. It has an immense distribution, being found over nearly the whole of the tropical and temperate parts of the Atlantic, the Mediterranean, the Indian Ocean, and such widely remote points of the Pacific Ocean as California, Australia, and New Zealand.

The blue shark is characterised by the very long pointed snout, nearly as long as the distance between the eye and the first gill-opening, the presence of a nictitating eyelid, the pectoral fin long and falciform, extending to the dorsal, which is nearer to the ventrals than to the root of the pectorals, the tail and caudal fin long and slender; the teeth are large, and have a single sharp cusp, those of the upper jaw oblique, scarcely constricted near the base, those of the lower jaw triangular in young examples, lanceolate, with a broad base, in old ones; the teeth of specimens about 4 feet long have a distinctly serrated border, but this serrature is lost in old examples. The upper parts are of a deep blue, the sides and the belly white, the fins dark, the pectoral nearly black.

This species is viviparous, and the young, measuring about 2 feet, are born in June, according to Couch;

57.—THE SPANISH MACKEREL.

58.—BLUE SHARK.

the mother is said to look after her young. Extremely voracious, like all sharks, these fishes are also very tenacious of life, and Couch mentions one which, having been thrown into the sea after its liver had been removed, pursued and tried to secure a mackerel.

The porbeagle [1] (*Lamna cornubica*), which grows to a length of 10 or 11 feet, is of plumper form than the blue shark, its snout is shorter, the gill-clefts are larger, the eye lacks the movable lid, the caudal peduncle bears a keel on each side, and the teeth are very different, narrower, lanceolate, and always with smooth edges, but with a small basal cusp in large examples. The fish is grey or blackish above, and white beneath.

The porbeagle is a regular summer and autumn visitor to our west coast, and specimens are frequently taken on other parts of the English coast and in Scotland, as well as in the Orkneys and Shetland. The range of distribution, though not quite so extensive as that of the blue shark, is wide enough, as besides the North Atlantic and Mediterranean the species is on record from California —where it is said to be not rare—Japan, and New Zealand. This shark is also viviparous, as many as fifteen embryos having been found in a female ; but nothing precise is known of its breeding habits. It is a swifter swimmer than the blue shark, and several individuals usually join company in pursuit

[1] This name, first applied by Borlase in his "History of Cornwall," is a compound of porpoise and beagle.

of the herring-shoals, which suffer greatly from its depredations ; all sorts of fish and cephalopods form its food, but it is said to be partial to rough-skinned fishes, such as dog-fish and John Dories. It emits a very disagreeable smell, and its flesh is never eaten, except in Spain and Italy.

Shark-fishing affords sport on the coasts of Florida and California, when there is no tarpon or tuna to be got. In these warmer seas, the monsters which attract most attention are the hammerhead (*Sphyrna zygæna*) and the saw-fish (*Pristis*). The former is a shark true enough, but the latter, in spite of its general appearance, is classed in the ichthyological system with the rays, its gill-openings being entirely on the lower surface of the body.

59.—SHARK FISHING IN FLORIDA.

CO.—THROWING FROM THE SHORE.

CHAPTER XXV

SEA-FISHING: INTRODUCTORY

By F. G. AFLALO

LITTLE by little the sport of sea-fishing is attracting the attention in this country that has so long been accorded to its claims elsewhere. In almost every Mediterranean country long rods have for ages waved over rocky pools for bass, and horse-hair lines have hauled grey mullet from behind the surf that breaks on sandy shores. In Australian seas the trumpeter and schnapper, and at the Cape of Good Hope the snoek and steenbras, have afforded sport to the white man ever since he settled in those southern regions.

For some reason or other, however, probably in great measure because his lakes, broads, and rivers gave such excellent sport before they were unquestionably overfished, the Englishman at home did not avail himself of the opportunities on his own coasts until a comparatively recent time. It has been said that scientific salmon fishing as now practised was an unknown pastime forty years ago; and it may with quite as much accuracy be asserted that scientific sea-fishing, as expounded by "John Bickerdyke" and others, is a development of the last fifteen years. Much has been done to popularise it during the ten years that have elapsed since the inauguration of the British Sea Anglers' Society, but even now its recognition is only just becoming general. When I was a schoolboy—no great time ago, as time goes—sea-fishing for pleasure meant hanging a lead that would have looked well on a grandfather's clock over the side of a boat, on a coarse brown line, and catching, at intervals of some minutes, a dab or whiting of about half the weight of the lead. In those intervals some one in the boat was generally sick, so that the *Punch* caricatures of the early 'eighties were not far wide of the mark. The chief expense of the amateur sea fisherman in those days was usually the half-crown an hour which he paid to his boatman—a boatman, by the way, and not as a rule a fisherman. He used that worthy's tackle, and the bait was included in the exorbitant charge. Nowadays the enthusiast spends on his sea-tackle very little less than the salmon fisher; indeed, since tarpon and tuna are in every sense of the word sea-fish, and their capture in consequence sea-fishing, he may be said, under certain

61.—IN HARBOUR.

62.—*TWO CHAMPION BASS.*

conditions, to spend more. To some extent the lateness with which sea-fishing has taken its proper place among sports at home may be due to the comparative lack of large sporting fish on our coasts. Compared with the tarpon and tuna and sea-bass weighing hundreds of pounds, which anglers take on the rod off the coast of Florida or California, our bass and pollack, and even conger, are pigmies. At the same time, we cannot nowadays permit ourselves to be as difficult to please as the Brobdingnagians, who forbore to catch the fish of their coasts because they were no bigger than those of European seas. Nor can our sea fish be regarded as altogether too insignificant for the average ambition. As a case in point—though the recital of personal exploits is a little out of place here—I may, in passing, mention two bass, weighing respectively 9 lbs. and 11 lbs. 5 oz., which I caught, in the order given, on two consecutive mornings last July in a Devon estuary. Of such bass-fishing in the tidal waters of rivers more will be said presently, but these are merely cited in order to show that there is sport to be had in our seas by those who will look for it in the proper way. Both of these fish were taken with live bait on a pliant 10-foot fly-rod, with the lightest of gear, and, since the water was crystal clear, forty or fifty yards away from my boat. Those who have fished in tidal estuaries will know the sport to be had out of an 11-lb. fish on a trout-rod, and at the end of fifty yards of fine line before even starting on its first rush, then fighting gamely every yard of the

way in a five-mile tide rushing beneath a bridge.
I certainly did not consult my watch on the occasion, nor had I any thought to spare for the town
clocks that may have struck during that struggle;
but I know pretty well, from the times of two
Great Western fast trains, which sped by in either
direction while the bass and I were deciding who
was to be master, that the fight could not have lasted
much less than five-and-thirty minutes. As the
bass and its smaller fellow now repose, along with
the treacherous hook that proved the undoing of
both, behind my writing table, it will be surmised
that the fortunes of the day went as I should have
wished. And if the capture of two such bass on
two days running is not sport, then I do not know
what is. This luck—I do not for one moment
claim it as anything else—is exceptional, it is true,
but the rarity of such angels' visits nowadays lends
them an added charm.

Perhaps the best plan of division for the notes
that follow will be one which to every sea fisherman
of experience will suggest itself as the obvious. It
has not indeed the merit of novelty, for one angling
writer at anyrate—my friend " John Bickerdyke,"
in his admirable " Letters to Young Sea Anglers,"
in the later edition of which the element of youth
has been erased from the rubric—has previously
adopted it. Novelty, however, is not everything
where precedent is excellent, and I shall therefore
divide these remarks under two heads : fishing from
a boat, whether a rowing or a sailing boat; and

fishing from a fixed position, such as a pier or
harbour, an uncovered reef of rocks, or a beach of
sand or shingle.

Either of these may have its advantages. Leaving
aside for the moment the all-important consideration of temperament—I mean, in respect of the
most vulgar, but also most distressing, of marine
maladies—there can be no doubt that a boat of
some kind is the royal road to sport in the sea. It
gives the angler command over so vast an expanse
of water, and, unless he be so unhappily constituted
that its movements simultaneously deprive him of
command over himself, he will be able to operate
on deep-water shoals of fish at which the squeamish
landsman must helplessly gaze, as Napoleon gazed
at this unconquered island from the sands of
Boulogne. In a few, a very few, cases a boat
offers little or no advantage, or may even be less
convenient than a quay or pier. Such fish, for
instance, as smelts and grey mullet, which at certain
seasons browse alongside weed-grown docks, or, again,
the spring shoals of leaping bass that feed greedily
in the sunlit, rainbow-hued surf right up to a jagged
line of rocks, are cases in point, for, on the one
hand, the boat would give less chance of sport than
the quay, being likely indeed to disturb the fish,
and in the case of bass playing close to rocks, the
use of a boat might be actually dangerous. There
is a third case, that of winter cod and whiting
feeding just behind the breakers on the open East
Coast, in which beach-fishing not only has obvious

advantages over boat-fishing, but is generally indeed the only course open to those who seek these fish at that particular season.

These are, however, the exceptions; and fifty cases might with ease be cited in which the boat is by far the best method of reaching the fish, while in the vast majority of these, indeed, it is Hobson's choice. The capture of bass in a tidal river, already mentioned, is one; the pursuit of large pollack and sea-bream and sharks in deep water is a second; the taking of mackerel on moving baits, a very popular form of amusement in the summer months with those who like to catch a fish that is at once beautiful in life and not unworthy of attention on the breakfast table, and without much exertion or study of first principles, is a third; and these may suffice by way of illustration, as I must soon proceed from ethical generalisations to practical details.

There is one piece of advice which, with all diffidence, I want to offer here at the commencement. I have never tendered it before, because it seemed too daring, until surmise became conviction, and conviction was again and again borne out by actual result. I do not think any one else, at any rate quite recently, has offered it, nor, for one moment, do I think that any one will take it, but it is this. Do not, O nervous reader, make up your mind that you are going to be seasick and forego the delights of sea-fishing without giving it and yourself a trial, and, if you have the courage, a second

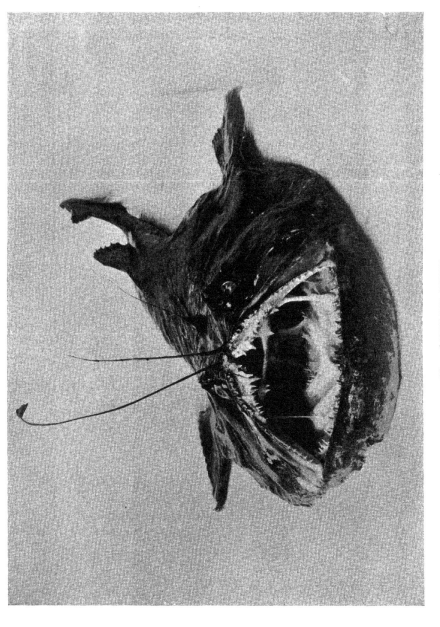

63.—ANGLER FISH.

64.— CORNISH PILCHARD.

trial after that. So many cases have come under my notice, since it was last my pleasant task to write at length on sea-fishing, of men, and ladies, too, for that matter, who were persuaded that they could never stand the least movement in a small boat, yet who, with a little brisk sport to distract their attention until their stomach and nerves had accustomed themselves to the new order of things, enjoyed themselves so much that they took to the sport with all the fervour of the convert, that I give the counsel for what it may be worth. Never having personally suffered the qualms of a complaint that is the curse of travellers and the inspiration of comic artists, my advice necessarily lacks a personal value. And yet I say : try, try, try again. It can, at the worst, only be a matter of a little determination. There will, of course, be extreme cases in which the first roll or jerk of the boat means collapse utter and complete, and individuals so constituted cannot, in mercy not only to themselves, but also to others in the same boat, do better than at once go ashore and stay there. Not for them, though, are the pleasures of angling in salt water, even from a boat, entirely proscribed. There are river estuaries in which bass and mullet, and even mackerel and conger, whiting and codlings may at the proper season be captured in water as calm as that of the morning tub. The two bass, that already threaten to emulate the revered head of King Charles, were taken in perfectly still water, at a point where the river is probably not more than a hundred yards at low water from bank to bank.

I shall, however, follow the division already indicated, and those who are resolved to keep away from the seductions of boat-fishing in deep water, must console themselves with such sport, at times excellent, as offers in landlocked "swims," as the roach-fisher would call them, and on either *terra firma* or some artificial continuation thereof. For the convenience, then, of the bilious—I have an affection for the orthodox word, though an eminent physician recently assured me that really bilious people are not subject to sea-sickness—the notes on calm water boat-fishing are given at the end of the first part, thus bringing them in close proximity to those portions which relate to pier and beach fishing. For strictly practical purposes, then, those to whom the frolic of dancing waves is anathema, may pass over the next fifty-six pages.

CHAPTER XXVI

SECTION I

SEA-FISHING FROM BOATS:
MACKEREL FISHING

By F. G. AFLALO

IT may be presumed, though the chronology and evolution of sea-fishing as a sport form no part of the scope of these remarks, that sea-fishing from boats came before sea-fishing from the shore. I neither expect this guess to pass without challenge, nor do I purpose setting forth at length the numerous arguments—based chiefly, I may say, on observations made at first hand in various parts of the

Mediterranean and in the East, where sea-fish were
caught and sold ages before Deal galley punts or
St. Ives' luggers were hauled up on the shingle
or run into harbour under reefed sails, according
to their several requirements. The arts of boat-
building having come comparatively late to the
assistance of early man, it might perhaps at first
sight look as if he had fished from the shore long
before he had fished from a boat of any description.
This may, it is true, apply to lake and river fishing,
where, more particularly in the latter case, bank-
fishing is, and always will be, the more popular
style with the vast majority. In the sea, however,
and more particularly in those Eastern seas dotted
with islands, and consequently affording choice of
calm lee water, where, moreover, the only fishes
to be caught as a rule immediately within the
surf are of the shark family, it seems to me
that shore-fishing came second. The point is of
historic interest rather than practical importance,
and need not here be laboured, but I suggest it,
for the benefit of those sportsmen who seek new
subjects of discussion for winter evenings, as an
improvement on the well-thumbed briefs and time-
worn pleadings in the matter of Mrs. Adder and
Offspring, Upstream v. Downstream Fishing, and
Velveteens v. Fox, and others.

Fishing from boats includes a great variety of
methods, differing according to whether the boat
is at rest or in motion. And here let it be said—
again in the interest of the sea-sick, for whom I

have a real affection—that it is only when the boat
is anchored in a choppy sea that they need really
be afraid of what they regard as disgracing themselves. (Personally, I do not see where the disgrace
comes in, for sea-sickness in a person who cannot
help being sea-sick is surely no more heinous than
blindness or deafness in those so disqualified.)
Mackerel fishing under sail, even in a sea tipped
with " white horses " and suggesting a horrible
dénouement, need have no terrors for them.

Let us take this same mackerel fishing first, since
it is for several reasons among the most popular
forms of the sport. For such general favour there
are many reasons not difficult to seek. The immunity from *mal de mer* is one. The ease with
which, when in biting mood, the gaily-coloured,
sporting mackerel are caught even by those who
have never fished before, not a dozen in an outing,
but thirty or forty dozen on good days, and the
welcome addition which they make to the table,
particularly when other fish is dear and not invariably fresh, all help towards an explanation of why
mackerel fishing takes precedence with the multi-
tude of summer seaside visitors over every other
kind of sea-fishing. For myself, let me confess it,
mackerel fishing, at anyrate in this way, has no
charms. I am not sea-sick ; I like a fish in proportion as it is difficult to catch ; and I very rarely eat
a fish that I have killed, chiefly because the only
half-dozen sea-fish really worth cooking well are
not, as a rule, cooked well in this country, and,

moreover, they do not in any case fall a victim to my hook more than once in ten years.

Still, these notes are intended for the benefit of the many, and let me therefore endeavour to give some wrinkles to those who would catch mackerel during July and August, when those fish are playing at the surface of summer seas and taking almost any and every bait offered at the end of a line.

The general principle of this style of mackerel fishing is to tempt the predatory shoals with moving baits. Fishes, like men, often prize that which they are about to lose, and our own misspent lives would doubtless yield, on investigation, many a counterpart of the callous mackerel awakened to a very frenzy by the sight of a glittering object wrested from its reach. Had the silvery inch of mackerel skin—the finest bait for these cannibals of the surface waters—lain at rest close to its pointed snout, no self-respecting mackerel would give it a second thought, and there it might lie till it sank deep enough to be swallowed by some small whiting or chad. The man who first discovered the secret of success with a moving bait would have been a genius, only there was obviously no such person, the art having been learnt in course of time in various northern lands. Movement belongs to the north; the south is happier at rest, and we do not find much of this use of moving baits in southern or eastern lands. The Hindoo catches his tank fish by hitching the line around his toe and going to sleep till awakened by the snatch of a rohu; the

Italian and Spaniard stand motionless on the rocks, or doze in their boats, yet rarely do they dream of moving their baits to and fro to incite the fish to a keener attack. Those more energetic forms of fishing, casting the fly and working the spoon or phantom, are of the north. They have found their way to the broad lakes and swift snow rivers that hide the great trout of New Zealand, a land of adoption that makes giants of a dwarf stock, but they were taken thither by the northerner.

Mackerel fishing with a moving bait may be practised from a sailing-boat or from one propelled more slowly by oars only. The former method is not only the more enjoyable, but also means taking about fifty fish to every one accounted for when the boat is rowed. The rowing-boat has only one advantage, and that is cheapness. It is very cheap. Its cheapest form is where the fisherman takes an unpaid friend to do the rowing—there are always friends with a passion for violent exercise in a temperature of 100°—and pays about ninepence an hour for the use of the boat. Even if his hour yields him only half-a-dozen mackerel, the fish and amusement together cannot be called dear at the price. A hired oarsman of the locality may increase the price of the boat by as much again in fashionable resorts, but the extra pay will not be thrown away if the man knows his work, for he will quickly find the mackerel and, once having found them, will so manœuvre his boat as to keep up with them, thus doubling or trebling the catch.

For mackerel fishing in this way from a rowing-
boat I should strongly recommend the use of a rod,
a 10-feet trout-rod for preference. It imparts an
element of sport to what is otherwise a not very
sportsmanlike style of fishing, and, what is more,
it may under certain conditions of wind and water,
enable the fisherman to hook many fish that come
short at the bait and that would consequently, but
for the elastic spring of the top joint, go free.
The rest of the tackle is not complicated. As to
the best kind of winch, or reel, fishermen are divided
in their opinions. There are many who swear by
the wooden Nottingham reel, that free-running,
optional-check contrivance which was evolved by
some genius on the banks of Trent, and which
is, like many another modern innovation, a good
servant but a bad master. In the hands of a
maître, delicately manipulated as I have seen it
manipulated by Mr. Alfred Shaw, the famous Notts
cricketer, who once gave me some much-needed
lessons in its use, the Nottingham reel is a marvel-
lous aid to fishing. Bungled, allowed to overrun
and generally abused, as I have seen it here and
there, in boats and on piers, it is a curse and a
delusion, and I would rather any day have a lively
conger in my boat than an angler with a Nottingham winch and a hundred yards of line that he did
not know how to manage. The Nottingham winch
offers undoubted advantages in sea-fishing, where
the great length of line constantly in use, either to
reach deep water or to trail at a distance behind

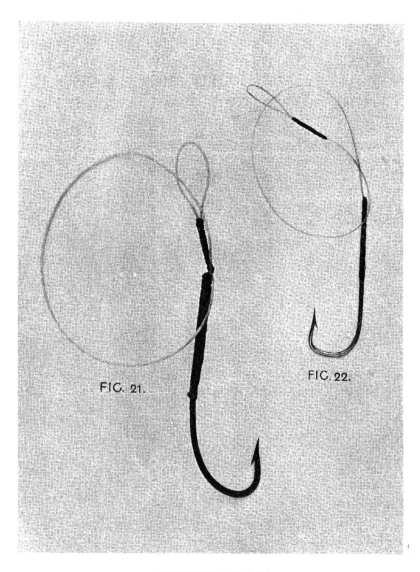

FIG. 21.

FIG. 22.

SPECIMEN HOOKS.

65.—COMMENCING OPERATIONS.

the boat, takes an unconscionable time winding in on the older bronze winches of smaller barrel. With a sea-rod indeed, which I use, as will presently be described, for catching pollack in deep water, there is nothing to beat a good Nottingham winch with optional check. It must be of the best, and it must have certain special qualities to fit it for use in salt water. Given these, and a man who can make it do exactly what he wants, it makes the odds against the fish very heavy. There is, however, a place for everything, and I do not think that the place for a Nottingham reel is on a trout-rod. At best, it would have to be small in the barrel, and this must necessarily lessen the rapidity with which the line can be wound up. Nor does the average trout-rod balance half so well with a wooden Nottingham winch as with the smaller and heavier bronze check winch more commonly used. Such a winch I prefer, and it may hold fifty or sixty yards of very fine dressed line. Such a line, if properly dried after use and given an occasional soaking in fresh water, should last the season out at least. The rest of the gear for this fishing consists of six feet of single gut, a couple of inches of lead foil, weighing perhaps an ounce, which may be pinched on the line just above the point at which it is attached to the gut, and a single hook of the size figured here (Fig. 21).

The choice of hook is largely a matter of opinion. As with most other things, with guns and cameras and rods, less depends on the tools than on the workman. One man pins his faith to round-bend hooks, another to square-bend; one kills more fish with a small, another with a large hook; one will have none but eyed hooks, another prefers the flattened shank used by the deep-sea fishermen. It is largely a matter of faith, and, just as many a man, who shoots brilliantly with his own gun, will go utterly off the mark with a better weapon which is strange to him, so, if a fisherman has accustomed himself to one pattern of hook, he will, if suddenly compelled to use another, lose fish after fish. Nor are one's preferences in these matters immune from change. There was a time when I used square-bend hooks above all others, but I first found the advantage of a round-bend in live-bait fishing for bass, and have since used the round hook for everything. The rod being put together, the reel fixed in place, the line through the rings, even the hook and gut attached and lead twisted up small and pinched on the line where previously indicated, there remains the question of bait. The best bait is undoubtedly, as already mentioned, a small ovoid piece of flesh and skin, chiefly skin, which is cut from either side of the tail, each fish supplying two baits. These baits, which go by a different name at almost every twenty miles along the coast, and which are known as "lasts" in Sussex, as "floats" in Devon, and as "snades" in Cornwall, are very deadly when properly cut, and one will, under favourable conditions, last long enough for the

capture of a dozen mackerel, as the fish is too
quickly hooked, at any rate from a sailing-boat,
to do much damage to the bait. The "float"—
I retain this name out of deference to Devon, where
I am writing these notes—requires careful cutting.
The requisite materials are a newly caught mackerel,
a very keen, broad-bladed knife, such as kept by
the fishermen for such uses, and an ordinary wine
cork. The mackerel being first killed, not only
on humane grounds, but also, it is to be feared,
because its movements would make cutting the
bait a very difficult job, is held in the left hand,
with either side uppermost. The blade of the
knife, with its edge towards the tail fin, is then
gingerly inserted in the skin a couple of inches
from the root of the tail fin, and, by diminishing
the pressure as the blade works along, it is, with
a little practice, easy enough to cut out a very thin
bait, semi-circular at the start and gradually taper-
ing to a long and threadlike point. Care is taken
not to cut into the flesh, for the bait should be
little more than skin, so that it works and spins
well in the water. The "float" must not be torn
abruptly from the mackerel, or its shape will be
spoilt; it must be quietly, but firmly, detached
with a turn of the knife. But of what use to give
these laboured explanations, which not a hundred
diagrams would elucidate half so well as watching
a fisherman do the job half-a-dozen times! Once
cut from the fish, the rest is easy. The "float" is
laid on the cork, skin side downwards, and the

point of the hook, which must be very sharp, is pushed through the tail, or pointed end. Then the bait is pushed with the thumb and finger down over the barb of the hook until it hangs from the bend, and, that being done, the baited hook may be let down over the side and line paid out from the reel until the hook is twenty or thirty yards astern.

Now, it will at once occur to the reader, particularly if he is an Irishman, that it may be necessary to catch your mackerel before you cut artistic baits out of the side of its tail. The "float" lasts so well, as already stated, that it is generally possible, in the height of the season, to catch the first mackerel with the dried-up baits of the days before, which a very little towing through the water restores to their first freshness. It may, however, very well happen earlier in the season that there are not even old "floats" available. In such a case, it is necessary to catch mackerel number one with some form of artificial bait. A large yellow-bodied "fly" with white wings and a little silver tinsel, such as supplied by Hearder, of Plymouth, and any other maker of sea-tackle, or one of the little tin spinners so familiar in the tackle shops, now that the sport of sea-fishing has compelled attention to its requirements, will answer the purpose admirably.

Once, however, the mackerel is caught, do not let reluctance to maim it tempt you to continue fishing with the artificial bait. However excellent such lures may be for the pollack of some locali-

66.—IN FULL SWING.

67.—*WELL INTO HIM*

ties, they are only second best, and a late second at that, for mackerel, and it is false economy not to change to the natural bait at the first opportunity. The hypercritical say that one side of the fish—the left, I think it is—gives a better " float " than the other, but when you find your boatman taking this line, especially if he knows that he will have the bulk of the fish to sell, do not believe him entirely, even though the air be salty, for his object is to prevent the fish being disfigured on both sides, such fish fetching a lower market price at most ports.[1]

Once the angler has put together his tackle, baited his hook, and paid out line, a good deal of what follows depends on the boatman, or on the convenient and inexpensive friend who takes his place in the bow. The first thing is to find the mackerel. For this there is no rule, but the experienced fisherman keeps a watchful eye on the movements of the gulls and other sea-fowl that prey on moving shoals. It is not, as a rule, the mackerel themselves on which the birds are intent, for they would prove too large and too active for anything but a gannet or cormorant to tackle. The mackerel, however, are themselves desperate characters, attacking the young rocklings

---

[1] Since writing these lines, I find that my friend, the late Mr. J. C. Wilcocks, also asserts (in " The Sea Fisherman," fourth edition, p. 126) this superiority of the left-hand " float." As I always had the greatest regard for him as a pioneer, and owe much, very much, to his correspondence, I hasten to qualify what is said above with an admission that the fisherman may, in this instance, probably be in the right.

and sand-eels and other surface-swimming fry,
harrying their shoals and leaping among them
open-mouthed in a manner that cannot fail to attract
rival fish-eaters from overhead. Just as in the desert
I have seen a single vulture drop from the "deep-
domed empyrean" on a fallen camel, and thereby
hail its watching comrades to the banquet, so the
swopping, crying gulls point the way to the uncertain
fisherman, and their tell-tale flight is a safe guide to
a good catch. Once the shoal is found it should be
no difficult matter, even in a rowing-boat, to catch a
score of fish. Let the oarsman pull his hardest—for
pollack, on the other hand, bid him go his slowest,
and he will not refuse—and keep a ready hand on
the winch. The moment the double tug of a
mackerel is felt, raise the rod top. Never strike
sharply, as the fresh-water fisherman strikes, when
using a pliant rod from a moving boat at sea, for if
by chance the biting fish should be a pollack, never
out of the question when trailing baits for mackerel,
the sudden extra strain would be likely, not so much
to part the gear, but, what is infinitely more distressing, to snap the top joint. By gently raising the
top, however, as if in firm protest against the flippant
dancing at the other end, the fish will be securely
hooked in nine cases out of ten. In the tenth case
it is better to lose your fish than to break your rod.
When the mackerel is fairly on the hook, it is as
well to get it to the boat as soon as possible. With
larger fish, such as bass and pollack, the sportsman
legitimately gets as much play as possible out of

them before bringing the proceedings to a close, but the majority of English mackerel are not sufficiently heavy to give very much play when the boat is under way. If only one rod is in use it is as well to let your man rest on his oars while you are bringing each fish to the boat, not merely to take the added strain off the light rod, but also to bring the fish in as quickly as possible and without creating a panic among the rest. When, however, more than one bait is out, this stopping for each fish may be the reverse of expedient, for, in the first place, the other bait may, in comparatively shallow water, go to the bottom as soon as the way is off the boat, and there get involved in differences with sharp rocks or cling-ing weed fronds, and, in the second place, the second bait, dragging through the water, is often successful in keeping the mackerel together in the wake of the boat. The mackerel, then, is reeled in as swiftly as possible, some little law being allowed to unusually large fish, and it will be seen that it sheers to right and left in narrowing circles as the line comes home. Small fish may be " hand-lined " out of the water, care being taken to choose a moment when the head of the fish points towards the boat, when a very slight jerk will lift it clear of the water and over the side. If, on the other hand, the angler is so incau-tious as to lift the fish at the moment when it is heading away from the boat, the parting of the fine gut will be a not improbable result. The strength of even a comparatively small mackerel in the water is almost incredible. Extra large fish, of a pound or more in weight, should be brought to the boat in a short-handled landing-net, as this will relieve the light tackle of a good deal of quite unnecessary and most damaging strain. The mackerel should not be allowed to fall in the bottom of the boat until the hook has been removed from its mouth. As a matter of fact, it should not be thrown in the bottom of the boat at all. A little attention to cleanliness and order, without spoiling the day's pleasure by anything approaching to fussiness, adds immeasurably to the comfort of such excursions. Let the mackerel, then, be caught deftly in the left hand and firmly grasped, while a single twist of the hook shank frees the point and barb from the throat of the fish. The back of the mackerel's head is then knocked smartly against the foot-rest or seat, and the dead fish is dropped in a box or basket placed handy for the purpose. The " float " is pushed back into position, on the bend of the hook, and the message of invitation goes back to the shoal that, it may be hoped, hangs around the boat with a friendly invitation to " drop them a line."

From mackerel fishing with such delicate tackle from a rowing-boat to mackerel fishing with somewhat heavier gear from a boat sailing three or four miles an hour is but a short step. The distinction —which is generally drawn in books by describing the lighter work as " whiffing," and the heavier as " railing " or " plummetting," the latter being a Cornish term—is mainly that of heavier leads and a hand-line instead of a rod. Personally, on the rare occasions on which I do indulge in this style of fishing, chiefly when fresh bait is wanted for the pollack farther out, I use just the same light gut gear in combination with a "plummet" of Cornish pattern, which is simply a solid cone of lead having a longer and shorter loop of strong waxed line let into it. To one loop is attached the line, to the other, preferably with an intervening fathom (six feet) of finer line, the gut collar or trace. As to the line between the hand and the lead, there is not only no particular object in having it very fine, but it is positively undesirable. The fish pay attention only to the line beyond the lead, and a thin line held in the hand soon cuts through to the bone under the constant strain. Even a thicker line, while less likely to chafe the skin, may become unpleasant after an hour's fishing, and a pencil, or, better still, one of the boat's tholes, is far more comfortable to hold, the line being hitched round it. The length of light line beyond the lead varies, as does also the weight of the lead itself, with the thickness and position of the line if several are in use at the same time. Those who fish for the market will use six or eight mackerel lines from each sailing-boat, some being worked from the end of great outrigged booms that project like limbs from the sides of the boat, while others are worked inboard. The lightest line is always worked from the stern of the boat, by way of lessening the chances of fouling, and the lead, which may weigh a pound or even a little less, according to the strength of the breeze and conse-

quent pace at which the boat sails, is about twenty
feet from the hook. The next heaviest lines come
amidships, and these carry a lead of twice the weight
only fifteen feet or less from the hook. The heaviest
lines of all are used for'ard, and in these the lead
may weigh as much as three pounds, while the
distance between it and the hook is no more than
nine or ten feet. These weights and measures have
been most carefully worked out as the result of the
experience of generations of clever and ingenious
fishermen anxious to work as many lines as possible
from each boat without the constant fear of entanglement, and they may be taken as, on the whole, the
best that can be adopted. The method of taking
mackerel on hand-lines out of a sailing-boat differs
slightly from the rod-fishing just described. It is
found an advantage to keep the lead and hook
swinging in the water, which is done by moving the
arm to and fro, and thus pulling the lead a foot or
two forward and letting it go back again, this movement being performed perhaps half-a-dozen times a
minute, sufficiently fatiguing exercise, but at times
very well worth while. Much depends on the way
in which the fish are feeding. If they are very
ravenous, one fastens itself on to the hook every few
minutes whether it be kept swinging or not; but at
other times, when they are biting short, the swinging movement will catch many that would otherwise
be lost.

Such is mackerel fishing under sail. Can it be
called sport? Well, seeing that sailing itself is

called sport—as are also mountaineering, diving, and the driving of a motor car—the name may perhaps be applied without hesitation. Yet where the sport comes in it would be difficult to say. The essence of sport, or of enjoyment in sport, is some difficulty, greater or less, overcome, and there can be no difficulty in periodically hauling in forty or fifty yards of line with a comparatively small fish, half-drowned by the rate at which it is pulled through the water, at the other end of it. The novice and the skilled hand are on a par, and there is no reason why the one should hook more fish or fewer than the other. And yet, as I have already said, in spite of these considerations, or perhaps because of them, mackerel fishing in this way is the pastime that attracts more people who visit the coast in the summer months than any other of the kind. The popular taste is being educated in its sea-fishing, but the education has not gone very far, and the fastidiousness is not marked. So long as plenty of fish are caught, particularly if the fish are good to eat, most people don't much mind how they catch them. Lying back in a sailing-boat and dancing up and down a picturesque coast is so much more agreeable than anchoring in a tumbling sea eight or ten miles from land, seen from which distant point of view all the coastline merges into an ill-defined grey line. So it is, and small blame to those who have the courage of their opinions and frankly own their preference. Yet it is yachting rather than fishing, and should be classed as such.

It is as if a man were invited to a covert shoot and should ask to be allowed to sit on the sunny side of a hill, smoking his pipe, and shooting such stray birds or rabbits as should come his way.

There is, however, another style of mackerel fishing which, to my way of thinking, is infinitely preferable, and that is drift-line fishing from an anchored boat. In order that this shall be successful, the mackerel must be abundant, and also widely distributed in the locality. It will not do if there are one or two large shoals only roaming about the coast. That condition of things answers the purpose well enough when one fishes from a sailing-boat, for it is not a matter of great difficulty to sail about until the fish are found. When, however, it is a case of the fish coming to the fisherman instead of the fisherman going to the fish, it is of importance that the latter should be found almost anywhere in the bay or open sea, as the case may be, opposite the port from which the angler starts. Given sufficient fish and calm weather, this drift-lining for mackerel is very pretty work. The boat may be anchored a mile or two from shore; if on a well-known mackerel ground, generally at the edge of a reef of rocks; or in a spot where the fish are actually known to be at the time, so much the better. They will not be seen at the surface, nor are the movements of the gulls of much use, because drift-lining is practised only late in the summer, when the shoals have broken up and the fish are feeding nearer the

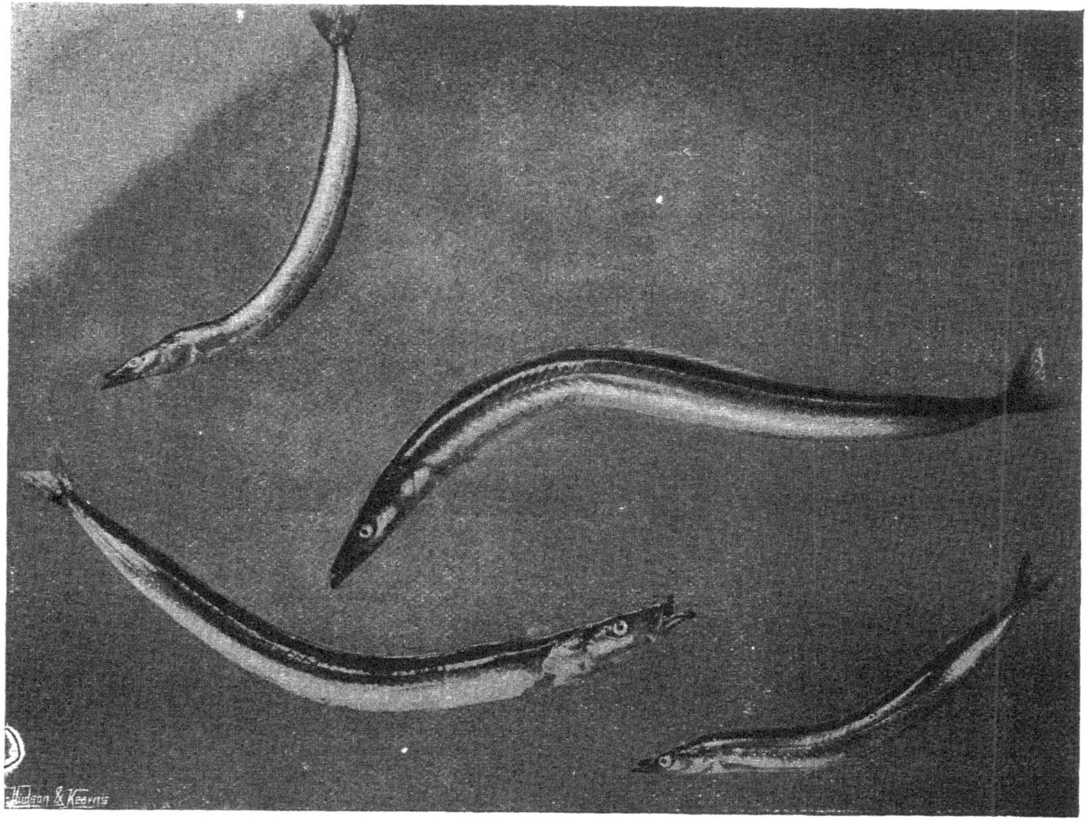

68.—LAUNCE AND SAND-EEL.

69.—PLUMMETING FOR MACKEREL.

bottom. As a matter of fact, the drift-line takes a larger class of mackerel altogether, fish of an earlier year, but these are not taken alongshore in this way until the end of July or beginning of August, though the surface lines may catch fish as early as the latter days of May. The only sea-birds that I have found any guidance as to the movements of these drift-line mackerel are the cormorants and shags, which are sometimes seen paddling among the launce—eel-like fish not un-like sand-eels, on which both the cormorant and the larger mackerel and bass greedily prey—and which may generally be trusted as giving a pretty close idea of where the fish are. And the fish found by such a clue will also be feeding, a matter of im-portance, though the mackerel is perhaps less subject to interludes of abstemiousness than most others.

A little tide is essential for drift-line fishing, the principle of which is to anchor the boat in the tide-way, and let the line and hook, without any lead to weigh it down, drift away on the tide. The light line and gut tackle above described for whiffing from a rowing-boat will do admirably, though the lead may with advantage be removed. As these drift-line mackerel are larger fish as a rule than those caught on the moving lines, a more substantial bait is usually offered to them, a 3-inch strip of pilchard, mackerel, or fresh herring with the flesh attached, or a couple of medium-sized mussels, will be found to answer the purpose. This drift-line

fishing is very sporting work with a trout-rod, but
I have also enjoyed it at times even more with a
very light hand-line. Striking at exactly the right
moment with a light drift-line held in the hand is
a fine art that can only be acquired by long practice,
and the only method of hand-lining that I know to
be even more artistic is that employed by Australians in fishing for black bream. So delicately
do the larger bream bite, so quick must be the
angler's response, that colonial fishermen are said to
wear away the skin on the inside of the thumb and
forefinger in order to render it more sensitive. We
do not proceed to quite such extremities in fishing
for mackerel, but certainly the striking, though not
rough, must be quick and direct ; and I have known
ladies, who are naturally more delicate-handed as a
rule than men, catch far more fish in this way than
he who took them out and taught them how. As
it is necessary to strike so promptly, the drift-line
must, if there is to be any certainty of success, be
held in the hand, and it is not therefore advisable
that each person should fish with more than one.
If, however, it is desired to use others not held in
the hand, the only way is to hitch these on to a
small cork bung, which lies in the bottom of the
boat, to which, with a lot of slack line, it is also
made fast. When a mackerel runs away with the
bait, the cork bung is dragged overboard, not only
drawing the angler's attention to the runaway line,
but also, when it strikes the water, causing a
momentary check that generally ensures the fish

hooking itself effectually. It is always important that the point of the hook should be kept very sharp, but if there is any kind of fishing in which this is doubly important, it is mackerel fishing. A blunted hook in mackerel fishing means failure, and nothing but failure, for these fish are all dash and hurry, and there can be no question of gorging the bait. Unless a mackerel is firmly hooked in the first moment, it will not be hooked at all, and the antics of a mackerel badly hooked and missed are generally sufficient to send the rest of the shoal on a cross-Channel swim.

Small living sand-eels are also excellent bait for these large mackerel, though they are not always procurable. The hook is passed through the lower lip, then, with a twist, just caught in the skin of the throat. The gills must not be touched, else the breathing will be impeded and vitality will soon ebb, and it is also important not to thrust the hook too deep, as such a bait should last from ten to twenty minutes, or, in cool, fine weather, even longer.

The mackerel has somehow occupied a considerable number of pages, but I do not regret this, for, whatever one may think of the orthodox sailing after them, or rather before them, as a form of sport, there can be no two opinions as to the game qualities of these fish. If only they grew to the size of bass and pollack, mackerel would be the only fish worth fishing for in our seas. They would not, however, be easily exterminated, for I doubt whether any ordinary light tackle would hold them. On some coasts the largest mackerel, like the largest conger, are caught at night. In this case the drift-line method is used, and if there is a strong spring-tide running, a few little pipe leads, which are modelled on the pattern of a clay pipe stem, and which may be purchased weighing from a quarter of an ounce to a pound, may with advantage be used at intervals along the line. It must, however, be borne in mind that such an addition of lead robs the line of much of that lightness that at once conveys the finest bite to the alert hand; and the smallest sizes, half an ounce each at most, will be found sufficient for the mackerel lines, though for bass or pollack leads of two or three ounces may not be too heavy in the tideway.

CHAPTER XXVII

SEA-FISHING FROM BOATS:
POLLACK FISHING

By F. G. Aflalo

Bass and pollack are, in fact, the other fish caught
by the methods already recommended for mackerel,
though with heavier tackle in proportion to their
greater size and strength. In fishing for them with
moving baits, however, the rowing-boat is not only
the better craft, but it is the only one, for the
additional strain of such heavy fish would be too
great on lines moving rapidly after sailing-boats.
As it is, the mackerel fisher now and then loses all
his finer gear at the end of the main line by a
prowling pollack taking a fancy to the bait. Moreover, the sailing-boat, apart from the disadvantage
above named, has another drawback; it moves too

fast for, at any rate, the pollack, which, though a predatory fish, makes its raids in somewhat leisurely fashion. Whiffing for bass or pollack, then, must be done from a rowing-boat. The only alternative is a motor launch, the speed of which can be made as slow as is required without any reference to the wind. It will be said that a sailing-boat can also be sailed slow, which in a measure is true. But a sudden puff of wind may put a correspondingly sudden strain on the line at the very moment when there is a heavy fish at the other end, and the result of such a combination would inevitably be disaster.

There are parts of the coast, as in the deep water off the Lizard, where this method of catching bass is in favour, and there, I believe, it yields excellent results. It has not, however, come my way, and my preference when writing on these matters is to describe them at first hand. Whiffing for one large fish is much the same as whiffing for another, nor, indeed, save in the employment of stronger tackle and larger hooks, does it appreciably differ from whiffing for small fish. Virtually, then, what has been said of whiffing for mackerel applies for the most part to the capture of bass or pollack by the same method. The only important distinction is that the bass is a fish of quicker movements than the pollack, and it also feeds, as a rule, nearer to the top of the water. This being the case, the bait must move more quickly for bass than for pollack, and also nearer to the surface. The way to increase the

speed of the bait is obviously to increase that of
the boat. The regulation of the depth at which it
moves through the water is a somewhat more com-
plex arrangement, depending as it does on several
co-related conditions. Other conditions being equal,
the heavier the leads on the line the deeper it would
sink. With the leads a constant factor, it would
sink deeper as the boat went slower. Any one who
has hauled in a leaded line behind a boat that moves
knows that the lead comes to the surface as it is
hauled faster. Lastly, if the other two conditions,
the speed of the boat and the weight of the leads,
are equal, the bait will sink lower in proportion as
a greater length of line is let out. There are,
therefore, these three methods of keeping the bait
at the greater or lesser depth : putting more or less
lead on it ; rowing the boat faster or slower ; and
letting out a longer or a shorter line.

Where the pollack run large, that is to say
anything over 6 or 8 lbs., a short spinning rod
and trace of twisted gut will be found advisable,
and with this the Nottingham reel is a boon. With
smaller pollack, however, where the largest fish is
5 lbs., more sport will be had out of a trout-
rod and bronze winch as recommended for mackerel,
only the winch should hold at least eighty yards
of line, as the first downward rush of even a
5-lb. pollack makes considerable demands on fine
gear. The advantage of the Nottingham winch,
even where it is not necessary to cast from it in the
approved way, is that the line runs out freely,

whereas any one using the check bronze winch
has to pull line off until there is as much out as
required.

In whiffing for pollack a knowledge of the ground
over which you are rowing is necessary, for these
fish are found over rocks only. To some extent
also this applies to whiffing for bass, but the
bass, like the mackerel, also feeds on the sand.
It is, of course, in fishing at anchor that this knowledge of grounds, or "marks," is of paramount
importance. In whiffing, after all, the boat moves
over a deal of water, and if the fish are not found
in one place, they will be in another. When at
anchor, however, an even slight mistake may be
fatal to success, for the fisherman may, without
any warning sign beyond his ill-luck, be patiently
dangling baits over one spot while the fish are
congregated and hungry on another not fifty yards
distant. If the current sets from the fisherman's
boat to them, there is some chance of the oily
particles from his bait floating along the tide and
attracting the fish to his hooks; but if, on the other
hand, the current flows from the fish past the hooks,
the case is hopeless.

However, the local fishermen generally know
these marks pretty well, and they need not be
too strictly adhered to in whiffing so long as the
boat is over rocky ground. The great art of this
whiffing, particularly when the pollack are feeding
deep, is to keep the bait just on the move without
getting it hung up in the rocks. When the ledge

70.—SEA BREAM FISHING OFF THE EDDYSTONE.

is a flat one, modelled on a coral reef, the difficulty is not great ; but when the rocks are uneven and are, moreover, thickly grown with "boot-lace" weed, the chances of a foul are considerable. A few lobster pots in the neighbourhood, with their attendant corks and ropes, afford the fisherman additional opportunities of showing the skill with which he can manœuvre his hook clear of such obstacles.

So far much has been said of the tackle and mode of fishing, and nothing of the baits. These may be either natural or artificial. The choice rests with the angler, and depends on various conditions. One of these is the absence of live bait. In that case the angler obviously either uses artificial or stays ashore. When live bait, particularly the living sand-eel, is to be had, it always takes precedence with me over the most cunning artificial baits ever modelled, though I have had excellent sport with the Plymouth band baits and with the rubber eel, and there are numbers of pollack fishers, who probably know a good deal more of the fish than I do, who prefer the artificial baits at any price. There is this difference, of course, that the rubber baits must, to give them a proper spin, be towed behind the boat, whereas the living sand-eel can be paid out on the tide, its natural movements giving it an attractive spin in the water, while the boat is only just kept moving with an occasional dip of the paddles. It may perhaps be objected that this method is not whiffing, but approximates rather to the drift-line method already described.

Well, it is my business to put the reader in possession of the most killing methods of taking the chief sporting fishes of our seas and not to quibble about names.

Drift-lining is, in fact, also practised from an anchored boat for bass and pollack. The drift-fishing for bass in estuaries is quite different, and will be described in a later page. In drift-lining for pollack, as for mackerel, the boat is anchored out in the tideway, but always over rocks and often as far as ten miles from the coast. The tackle is much heavier than that used for mackerel, and the light rod is usually laid aside for a sea-rod. So little sport, however, have I lately found in these stiff rods that I have been using the hand-line whenever the trout-rod was *hors de combat.* Whether this is only a passing fancy, or whether it will crystallise with me as permanent doctrine, it seems desirable to record such impressions at the moment of writing. The bait for a pollack of 10 or 15 lbs. must be something worth offering to a fish of such splendid appetite, and the half of a large pilchard is not deemed too much. To those unfamiliar with a fish little known outside Cornwall, it should be explained that the pilchard is not unlike a herring, only it is a smaller, greener fish, with larger scales. The side of a pilchard, then, of 7 or 8 inches in length, cut with one rip of the sharp bait knife from behind the neck to the root of the tail fin, makes a capital pollack bait, and another good bait is composed of one strip of pilchard and another of mackerel. This is a particularly useful combination on days when the chad, or small red bream, are too attentive to the hooks. These little plagues, which afford endless amusement to the children that fish from the piers and quays, are a constant spoil-sport for the more serious angler out in deep water, and the extreme remedy is to put out a chad line with small hooks, catch one or two of the greedy little fish on a small bait of mackerel or pilchard, and then bait the pollack hook with a large slab of chad. This, while not perhaps as attractive to the pollack as the more oily pilchard bait, is nevertheless generally appreciated, and it has the further advantage of being very tough and resisting the constant worrying by other chads, which at once drag the soft pilchard bait off the hook.

Three fish are commonly taken on these drift-lines for pollack in the deeper offshore water : the pollack, for which they are baited ; the large bream, which give perhaps less sport, but are infinitely better for eating purposes; and the sharks, blue or porbeagle, which are useless when killed, but which certainly afford a measure of sport in the killing, with just a dash of that excitement inseparable from the very name of these marauders. Although huge sharks, weighing a hundredweight or two, are captured in the fishermen's nets in Cornwall, nothing of great size is ever taken on the hook. I have once or twice had all my line run out and then broken, much as would happen if I hitched the hook to a motor car about to start on a tour round the world, and I have suspected very large sharks, such as are known to inhabit our south-western seas. Frankly, however, I never had a glimpse of these monsters at the other end of my line, as I have often had in Australia and elsewhere abroad, so their weight and dimensions were mere surmise. I have, however, taken porbeagle sharks of close on forty pounds, and blue sharks of considerably over twenty, on the rod, and good fun they are as long as they fight. Once brought to the gaff, they are disgusting ; and if any sensation could ever bring me near to sea-sickness, it is that of sitting in a boat, on a blazing hot summer day, with the boat rising and falling on the remains of an Atlantic storm, and a newly killed porbeagle shark in close proximity. This unpleasant contingency is, however, averted, for once killed, and even in the killing, the shark is kept carefully aloof from the other fish, and is then strung up at the bow. The capture of a shark generally marks the interval between two good spells of fishing, the lull being the result of the terror inspired by these hideous monsters. Keeping the shark away from the eatable fish in the well of the boat may be simply a superstition, or contact might actually damage the better kinds. I do not know. What is, however, worth recording is that the rowhound, or rough-hound, a relative of the sharks, makes colourless patches on any whiting or pollack or similarly dark-hued fishes with which its wet skin may come in touch, and this bleaching property even seems to be possessed by the water that drips from it.

One of the most interesting of the many studies that suggest themselves to the contemplative sea angler is the difference in the behaviour of the many fishes hooked. The shark behaves more after the manner of the bass and mackerel, sheering away at the top of the water, confusing any one unaccustomed to its quick twists and turns and changes of mood, for it will first steer right away from the boat, making the reel scream and playing mischief with the rod top, and then, without warning, it will head with the same amazing rapidity for the boat. This, unless the angler has reeled in very carefully, leads to trouble, for it is only with the utmost difficulty that he can keep a tight line on a fish that is swimming towards him at a hundred yards a minute, with perhaps another rush in the opposite direction at any moment. All said and done, then, a shark of 20 or 30 lbs. affords a chance of sport for ten minutes or so, and the fact of the fish being useless when brought to the gaff ought not entirely to disqualify it as a sporting customer, though I was never able to agree with my esteemed friend, the late Mr. Matthias Dunn, who gravely suggested that sharkfishing would, if properly advertised, become so fashionable a sport as to draw hundreds of yachtsmen and anglers to Cornish resorts every summer. Tastes differ in angling, fortunately, as in most other modes of pleasure-seeking, but the thought of enthusiastic pilgrims performing an annual journey to that western Mecca to slay such scaly vermin will be a little too much for the gravity of the critical. We may take our sharks as they come, anathematising them when they rob us of valuable tackle and deriving what fun we may from their capture when the hook holds; but to go three hundred miles specially equipped for such work is not, I think, likely to occur to London anglers anxious for distraction.

The behaviour of a pollack when hooked is entirely different from that of any of the other fishes so far mentioned, different indeed from any other familiar fish in our seas. If the action of a shark may be compared with that of a runaway horse, the manner of the pollack fighting for dear life might approximately be represented by a large tom-cat slung on a light line out of a top window. It sinks to the bottom like a weight, struggling and kicking every yard of the way. There is no hesitation on the part of the fish, which has but one object—to get to the rocks as quickly as possible, and there, if possible, to cut asunder the cruel line. It is no part of these notes on practical fishing to inquire too minutely into the psychological aspect of a hooked fish, but I desire mildly to record my conviction, and to stand by it, that the pollack has this object in view. It has been objected that the fish would not know the result of drawing a line across a sharp edge of rock, and that its object in "boring," as fishermen call it, is merely to hide away under some rock—the rush of the wounded creature to its lair. It is quite possible that the first pollack that ever bored in this fashion did so out of sheer fright and agony, but it must have accidentally cut the line across a rock and regained its liberty. A second experience of the kind, or, if fishes have means of communicating their thoughts—as why should they not?—a comparing of notes with a friend similarly placed, would have confirmed the lesson, and in course of time pollack have instinctively acquired a knowledge of this means of escape. Whatever the motives of the fish, however, one fact is of practical interest to the angler, and that is that the pollack will, given the chance, sever the line against the rocks or against the edges of the mussel shells that grow over them. My own plan is to withstand the first rush of the fish, however heavy, and to keep it from the bottom at all cost. This, in twenty or thirty fathoms of water—a very usual depth on good pollack ground six or eight miles out—is not a matter of great difficulty. It necessitates the use of a stout sea-rod or of a hand-line. With such a rod, the Nottingham reel is put at the check, and, over and above this, the thumb is cautiously pressed against the flying rim ; this throws much of the brunt on the top joint, but the top joint of an 8-foot sea-rod can stand a good deal. With the hand-line the line is gripped just inside the boat, and has to fly out between the thumb and first finger of either hand, with a further friction against the gunwale. This checking of the pollack's first rush is not perhaps very artistic fishing, but it kills the fish.

Mr. Walter Shaw, of Salcombe, has a more interesting plan of letting it run unchecked. He never uses a rod of any pattern for this work, but hand-lines all his fish, letting them go right down to the rocks and then playing them afterwards. I have never fished with him, but imagine that he throws out plenty of slack line. It would, unless the fish contrived to double ingeniously round a sharp rock, be very difficult, if not impossible, to cut a very slack line in the manner indicated. Any one doubting this should endeavour to cut a piece of string lying on a table one-handed, holding the blade of the knife edge upwards between the string and the table. An old trout-rod — it would be wanton wickedness to use a new one for such work unless bought specially, for it will not be of much account for trout again—gives good sport with these large pollack, though a number of the fish get away. There must be sixty or eighty yards of fine line on the reel, for the first rush has to go unchecked. After that it is a toss-up whether the fish wins or the fisherman. In any case they both get a run for their money, which is the ideal of sportsmanlike angling.

A simple and workmanlike gaff should be used in getting these large pollack into the boat. Failing such an implement on board, it is best, at any rate in Cornwall, to let your fisherman stoop over the side and hook his arm round the fish. These men do a lot of pollacking single-handed, and they get in the way of heaving their big fish into the boat in that way. Whatever you do, do not attempt to lift the fish in, if over a pound or two, by the line. A pollack may not, to all appearance, have any fight left in it after the first rush or two, but a fish that looks all but dead may make a wonderful effort if carelessly hauled into the boat, and more fish will escape that way than any other. There is nothing clever in hooking a pollack, for the simple reason that it hooks itself. The art comes in when the fish is fighting downwards on a light line and the angler has to get it, single-handed maybe, into his boat. In such a case, I am not sure that a landing-net is not preferable to a gaff, the latter being very difficult to use in one hand while the other is holding the line. The worst of a landing-net for pollack is that it must be rather large and unwieldy to be of use, the pollack being a very long fish for its depth. This is not, however, the place in which to discuss the merits of gaff or landing-net, for each has its advocates as firm in their convictions as the supporters of preferential tariffs and free trade.

Mention was made above of yet another fish often taken on the pollack grounds, and that is the sea-bream. There are several kinds of sea-bream on our coasts, and they are particularly plentiful down in the south-west, being, in fact, southern types. This is the common red sea-bream, very like the Australian snapper, and a fine fish it is, to fight first and then to eat. A bream of about a pound or a little less is known in Cornwall as a "ballard," a term of which I do not pretend to know the derivation, and in its still smaller stage, it goes, as we have already seen, by the name of chad. It is at all stages a bold biter, and few fish fight better for their weight.

I have just used the expression "pollack grounds," from which it will be surmised that this fish has its favourite haunts, and that, in order to catch pollack it is first necessary to find them. The fact is that the greater number of fishes caught from anchored boats must be sought on special grounds of their own, the position of which has from time immemorial been known to the professional fishermen of the locality. The only form of fishing at anchor in which this careful locating of the ground is not strictly necessary is the drift-line fishing for mackerel already described, and even in that there are sometimes favourite grounds. Still, if the fish are fairly plentiful, it is not usual to lose much time in picking up the marks. In fishing for pollack, however, for whiting-pout, for silver whiting, for conger, or in fact for any other fish with fixed haunts, it is not only worth while to put the boat over the ground with extreme accuracy, but it is of little use attempting to fish without doing so. If there were only two hours to fish in, it would be better to spend an hour and three-quarters, if necessary, in finding the exact spot and fishing for the remaining fifteen minutes than to hurry the man in anchoring and devoting most of the time to fishing on a chance ground. And how, it may fairly be asked by any one new to the work, how can one find with any certainty the exact position of a small reef or rocks lying at the bottom of a hundred and fifty feet of water, and situated five or ten miles from the coast? Well, the operation does not entail any great mystery, consisting only in the taking of careful bearings. The more bearings the amateur takes of any spot, the more accurately will he pick up the desired mark, but the fishermen often make shift with two. And what are these bearings? Why, simply imaginary lines drawn from the spot where the fish are to different points on the shore, and there prolonged so as to get one or more familiar objects in line. The principle is easily illustrated. If, for instance, any one were sitting in a boat a hundred yards or so to the west of Bournemouth pier and another hundred yards farther out, and if he looked straight ashore, he would see the red steeple of the Presbyterian Church over one of the chimneys of the clubhouse on the sands. If his gaze next fell on the flagstaff on the pier head he would find that it came under a building just beyond the Bath Hotel. Looking westward, he would find that he could just see a dark patch of gorse on the farther side of the first chine. And it goes without saying that if, storing these positions in his memory, he were to anchor his boat the next day in such a position that these points again coincided, then the boat would be over precisely the same spot. This is a simple case, for it presents no difficulty to any one with good eyesight and a fairly retentive memory, and even these gifts of the gods may in a measure be supplemented by a pair of binoculars and a notebook and pencil. When, however, it comes to picking up outside grounds, seen from which the coast is but a hazy line, it takes a professional eye to read off the bearings with accuracy. Anything in the nature of a detached rock standing away from the main line is invaluable in getting bearings, and the Gwingeas Rocks at Gorran, in Cornwall, are utilised in locating half-a-dozen different marks wide apart. The greatest exactness of all perhaps is required in anchoring the boat for whiting-pout, or "bibs," as they call them in Cornwall. These bold-biting fish, which may grow to a couple of pounds or rather more in weight—and they are then very different fish from the puny examples caught in thousands from our piers—congregate in gullies in the rocks. Unless the baits are lowered in these gullies, not a "bib" is taken, and as these gullies are mere crevices between two rocks, it will easily be imagined that great accuracy is necessary in mooring the boat exactly over the right spot. Two hooks are generally used in this pout fishing, the baits being pieces of mackerel or pilchard, and the fish are struck the moment they bite. The bite is conveyed to the fisherman as a wriggling movement lasting about two seconds, and during the two seconds he must strike sharply, or the fish and bait will both be gone. Pout are so clever at removing the baits that it is useless to leave the hooks down after missing a bite for each, as they are almost sure to be bare. If fishing with a rod, it is best to hold the rod in the right hand and the line between the thumb and forefinger of the left and, on feeling a bite, to pull about a foot of line smartly back through the rings. With a hand-line, hold the line inside the boat and, when the bite comes, pull it smartly down across the gunwale or edge of the boat. Merely jerking the rod top on the one hand, as you would strike a roach, or, on the other, hanging your hand out over the boat and pulling the line upwards, would not be sufficient if pout were biting delicately in deep water. As soon as you feel that the fish is hooked—on good days pout come up two at a time almost as often as one— haul in and do not pause for an instant till the pout is safely in the boat. A moment of slackness, and it will go to a certainty. You will generally catch, along with pout, at any rate on the deep-water grounds, a sprinkling of another fish not unlike them, but distinguished by their bulging eyes, which seem to be enveloped in a crystalline transparent viscous covering. These are poor cod or power cod, and they are the babies of the cod family, being smaller in the adult stage than any of their relatives. I cannot say much for them as eating, though they are not bad when quite fresh. Pollack, on the other hand, are said by those who eat them to taste better on the second day. Personally, I would as soon almost eat them on the twentieth as on the first.

CHAPTER XXVIII

SEA-FISHING FROM BOATS:
WHITING AND OTHER FISH

By F. G. AFLALO

THERE is a tackle, known as the "sprawl" or "chopstick," of which some account must here be given. There are two "rigs" of this tackle, the Kentish and the Dartmouth. In the Kentish, the form seen along the coasts of Kent and Sussex, the lead is conical or pear-shaped, and through it, or immediately over it, is a transverse sprawl of wire. It is to the extremities of this wire that the hooks are made fast. The Dartmouth "rig" differs from this, for, instead of being made fast to the centre of the wire, the hand-line is attached to one end of it, the lead being fastened below. This has the effect of making the hooks stand out obliquely on a long trace of their own. In the Plymouth "rig" for whiting and other fish there is no wire bar at all. The hand-line is made fast to one end of a boat-shaped lead and the trace bearing the hooks to the other. This boat-shaped lead, which is the only one for ground-fishing or drift-lining in a strong tide in use in Cornwall, has to be cast out somewhat carefully to avoid fouling. In case I have not already alluded to the importance of this, it may here be mentioned that this particular tackle, though excellent if properly used, is very apt to get tangled. To avoid this, the lead is held in one hand and the hooks in the other. The hooks are cast out first and allowed to drift clear of each other with the tide, and then, and not until then, the lead is thrown out and against the tide, the line being allowed to run out slowly as it sinks towards the bottom. Any one watching a fisherman do this should be able to imitate him in the course of about five minutes. To describe it satisfactorily on paper would take a chapter to itself, and the foregoing suggestion of the proper mode must suffice.

Another fish caught principally from anchored boats is the silver whiting—the true whiting (as distinguished from the whiting-pout and whiting-pollack), the fish dear to doctors who have convalescents in their power. Incidentally, it may be mentioned that those ingenuous longshore boatmen who take summer holiday folk whiting

71.—WHITING.

fishing at fashionable seaside resorts anchor their boat on some handy reef of rocks, and let their customers catch small pout. If any one of the party should remark on the darker colour and stouter form, the boatman is ready with the answer that these are the rock whiting—just the same as the others, only—a little different! The truth is, that until the fall of the year the whiting keep on the outer grounds, and it doesn't suit these gentlemen to pull a boat four or five miles out and the same distance back. Small blame to them, but if they would occasionally speak the truth and give their employers a chance of paying double for a sailing-boat to catch the real thing, I fancy they would benefit.

In the late autumn, or in some years even in the early days of September, the whiting come close inshore, and are caught in numbers from the piers and beaches of our south-east and east coast, Deal, Lowestoft, Yarmouth, and Aldeborough being favourite resorts of the whiting fisherman. To-gether with the cod, they come in after the sprats. By the way, any one mentioning this little fish in some of the Devon seaside towns may be puzzled on being asked whether he means "London" sprats or not, the fact being that the true sprat, the cousin of the herring, is known by the latter designation, while by "sprat" pure and simple the Devon nets-man means the common sand-eel.

The best August whiting ground that I know is the Eddystone, though that is not as good as it was ten or fifteen years ago. To fish the Eddystone properly it is necessary to choose a fine night during the short, or neap tides—a moonlight night, with just a little breeze to take our boat out to the old lighthouse. We leave the Hoe pier at eight or nine in the evening and draw slowly out, with a professional from the Barbican to put the vessel on the right spot. By midnight or a little after we have taken up our berth, and there is nothing to do till daybreak. Some one in the party remarks that it would have been better to start later, but if we had done so, the very excellent ground we are on would have been occupied by one or other of the tall-masted fishing craft that have silently followed in our wake, their green and red lights revealing and yet concealing the rest of their dim forms. One by one they drop anchor all round us, and from this alone it is apparent that our man has chosen his spot with the knowledge that comes only of long experience.

At last there are purple gleams in the east, and the black veil of night seems to be pulled slowly off the face of the waters by a hidden hand down west, behind the Rame. The baits—chiefly herring, mackerel, and squid—are cut up, the lines are baited, and the heaviest leads are used, as the ebbing tide still runs quickly. We let down the leads till they bump on the ground, then withdraw them five or six feet, according to the distance between them and the hooks, the object being to keep the latter just clear of the bottom. As the tide is swift, though it will slacken every minute, it is necessary to make sure every few moments that the lead is still near the bottom, and this is done by keeping some slack line handy on the deck and every now and then touching bottom with the lead and drawing in the necessary length to take the baits just clear. Then the line may be hitched round a cleat or thole pin and held in the right hand. For whiting it is essential to strike as quickly as for pout, and with them also the hauling must be continuous or the fish will be lost. Indeed, but for the fact that the pout is caught on the rocks and the whiting on the hard sand, the two styles of fishing are much the same.

The whiting is in one respect the most agreeable fish to catch in our seas, and that is that it is perfectly clean and free from spines. It may be grasped in the left hand while the right removes the hook without any fear of being either wounded with spines, like those on the bass, or covered with slime, like the conger's, or with scales, such as come off the pout.

The fun may be furious for an hour, but the fish do not come at the hook as a rule much longer than that, and when half-a-dozen lines have taken their six or eight dozen good fish—a catch that, while not perhaps entirely satisfactory to those who have to sell their spoils at the Barbican in time for the London train, should content any amateur who is not a pothunter—it is advisable to stop fishing and make the most of the breeze back home.

Let me give one word of caution to any one with

business engagements who is tempted to try a night's whiting fishing at the Eddystone, as here described. It is a temptation that he would do well to resist, unless he makes arrangements for a steam tug to be in attendance next morning at, say, seven or eight. I have fished on a good many coasts, and the experience has brought me my share of acquaintance with the caprices of the winds, with enough at times to blow one to Jericho, and at others too little to fetch back to port a mile or two distant, yet never did I know a spot where the wind was more uncertain in strength and more fickle in direction than Plymouth Sound. Those who are on holiday bent need not trouble their heads, and the only precaution they need take is to be sure that their arrangements with the owner of the fishing-boat is inclusive, covering "act of God," &c., as in shipping agreements, and that they will not have to pay double just because there is no wind to get back. I have been kept fooling out at the Eddystone, gazing in vain and with much wasted rhetoric at the distant breakwater, while the train in which I ought to have been seated was half-way to London. One such experience is enough, and in future steam power will be good enough for me when returning from such excursions.

Conger fishing, another and distinct amusement, is also best practised from an anchored boat, though there are several piers and harbours from which moderately large conger are to be caught in August and September, and on the south-west coast there

are here and there opportunities of conger fishing.
from the rocks. Two conditions are requisite for
the capture of large conger—a rocky bottom and
darkness. Depth of water is not necessary, and I
have caught on the rod a conger weighing close
on 22 lbs. in little more than twelve feet of water.
That is by no means a large fish as conger run, but
it is enough for a rod. I would not recommend
that weapon for this fishing; I merely tried it on
that occasion, nine years ago, down in Cornwall,
and as the conger took about forty minutes to kill,
during which time it turned everything upside down
in the boat, putting out the candle lamp with a
flick of its tail, and thereby causing me and my
man to hammer each other in the dark with the
belaying pins that we had provided ourselves with,
it was an experiment that will not, so far as I am
concerned, be repeated. The tackle used for conger,
then, should be a hand-line, and the particular form
of lead used, as well as the arrangement of the
hook with respect to it, does not much matter, and
will be a question of taste. Some use a heavy weight
on the bottom of the line and have the hook above
the lead. The great disadvantage of this, to my
mind, is the risk of the lead rolling into a crevice
in the rocks and there getting stuck. It is within
the experience of all who have fished much for
conger that there is considerably more difficulty
in freeing the line in the darkness than there would
be by daylight, so that every precaution should be
taken against fouling. It is with this object that

I prefer personally to use in conger fishing a heavier edition of the tackle used in those parts for pollack or whiting—that is to say, the orthodox boat-shaped pattern of lead and the long fine snood below it. The lead must be heavy, as it is desirable that the bait should lie quite motionless on the ground, and only the inertia of a large lead can insure this condition being fulfilled. The hook should also be attached by very strong gimp or flax bound with wire. It is not necessary to use an immense hook, as some conger-fishers insist on doing. If the hook is well-tempered and sharp, one of the size previously figured for pollack should serve the purpose admirably.

The best bait for conger fishing is squid, and squid may usually be procured out of the trawl or seine-nets in the vicinity, a few pence paying for sufficient to bait several lines during a night's fishing. The squid must be cut open and cleaned of its ink, and this is a disgusting job that may, without envy, be left to your boatman. The essential of success in conger fishing is absolute freshness of the bait ; the least taint, and you might as well go home at once. It is also regarded as an advantage to hammer it until much of the natural stiffness is removed, and the bait is perceptibly softer than before, but I have not, to tell the truth, found this any particular gain. The clean fresh squid is cut in strips of about four inches in length, and through one of these the hook is passed three or four times, till the bait is firmly twisted on it. The line being all clear, the lead is swung against the tide after first throwing over the baited hook, a method of avoiding fouling with this Cornish gear that no amount of description or illustration can show. Yet the fishermen can teach it to you in five minutes or something less. The lead is allowed to run until it touches the bottom ; then, as was recommended in whiting fishing, it is drawn up again until, this time, the bait lies just on the bottom. As much of the success of conger fishing depends on adjusting this nicely, it is worth measuring the distance between the lead and the hook very carefully, in order to make sure that the latter will lie just on the bottom with enough slack line to make it independent of the swing of the lead. All this being duly attended to, the fisherman holds the line in his right hand and waits. Waiting is of considerable importance in conger fishing, and self-restraint is the lesson it teaches. The successful conger fisherman does not strike at the first nibble as he would do if the fish at the other end of the line were a whiting or a mackerel; he waits until the eel nibbles once, and perhaps twice, and then moves steadily off with the line. All this his hand feels with a little practice, and it is not until the line is creeping steadily off that he quietly, but firmly, tightens it, and then gives a sudden and powerful upward stroke. Such tactics will, in nine cases out of every ten, hook the conger fast, and if the tackle is trustworthy in every inch, the rest is only a question of time. Now and again it may happen that the conger contrives to get its tail twisted round a rock. The proper course to adopt in that case is to throw all the strain on

the line that it will bear, then suddenly to relinquish the hold and throw a yard or two of slack
overboard. This will generally induce the conger
to come out and show fight again. Whether the
fish assumes (if deduction be a faculty of fishes) that
the line is broken, or whether it is dislodged by
some sudden pain consequent on the removal of
the strain to which it has braced itself, I do not
know, but the result may be tested by any one who
finds himself in that predicament. There are other
baits suitable for conger fishing, and among them
may be mentioned mackerel, herring, pilchard, rock-
ling, and sand-eel. So long as any of these is perfectly fresh, it will tempt a conger if there is one
in the neighbourhood. In proof of the importance
of having conger baits perfectly fresh, I may mention
that, although squid is a better bait for this fish
than pilchard, I have nevertheless found conger
prefer pilchards just out of the sea to squid that
had been exposed to the air for an hour or two.
This I had an opportunity of proving on one occasion when we started conger fishing at about nine
in the evening, just before the pilchard boats had
started hauling their nets. We had squid bait, and
the squid had on that occasion been taken out of
a seine net about five in the afternoon. When we
had caught half-a-dozen conger one of the pilchard
drivers, with her nets half-hauled, passed almost
uncomfortably close to our little anchored boat,
and a friend of mine, a visitor on board for the
night, threw in half-a-dozen pilchards just shaken
out of the net. One of these was promptly used

as bait on one of the lines, and the congers, which were biting rather well, only looked gingerly at the squid bait on the other line, while the fresher pilchard lasted. When it was done—and six pilchards don't go far with hungry congers playing around—the squid bait went down well enough, but not before the congers had plainly shown their preference.

I have here described conger fishing as a night sport, and so indeed it is as a rule, though there is no reason why congers, large enough to give the amateur sport, should not be caught in daylight. I once took one weighing over 6 lbs. off Hastings pier in the middle of the day, but that was many years ago. Hastings pier is particularly well placed for these fish, which find suitable food and shelter in the small reefs of rocks that run out at intervals from the edge of the shingle to low-water mark or a little beyond. There used in those days to be very fair bass fishing, both from the pier (there was no second pier at St. Leonards then) and from the large stone groyne at the east end of the town; but whether the conditions are still as favourable I know not, for I have not fished at Hastings for eleven years. There are, however, signs of great activity among the amateur sea-fishers of that ancient town, and the recent second annual festival marked a distinct departure in the public recognition of the sport as a certain attraction for visitors. Large bass have lately been taken from the beach, a mode of fishing unknown there ten or twelve years ago.

There is a miscellany of flat-fish, such as plaice,

dabs, flounders, small turbot, and lemon soles, which are caught by the amateur on inshore grounds, mostly in the summer months and in company with whiting and mackerel, gurnards and weevers. The last-named should be given the order of the boot, since their spiny fins are capable of inflicting fearfully painful wounds. For catching these flat-fish a light rod and fine gut tackle is the best combination; and for bait either lugworms or mussels. The lugworms are either to be procured of the professional bait-sellers in the neighbourhood, or, failing that source of supply, they must be dug from the sand just above low-water mark. In some places they are very plentiful, though less so than in former years, and there is little difficulty in digging sufficient for the day's fishing. As a rule, however, each of the larger lugworms has to be dug for separately, by following down the tunnel bored by it in the wet sand, and some care must be exercised in procuring the rapidly burrowing worm without breaking its skin. A lugworm is not pleasant to handle, still less attractive is it when it has to be used as a bait; but there are few sea-fish that will not take it at one time or another, and there is no better bait for flat-fish.

The baits and hooks must be small, to suit the mouths of these fishes, and they must lie on or near the sandy bottom. The fish hook themselves, and the angler has only to get them to the boat and remove the hook. It may in passing be remarked that it is easier to get a hook down the throat of a flat-fish than back again, and if the angler has not many spare hooks on gut with him, he will have to exercise some little care and patience if he is to remove the hook from a plaice or turbot without breaking the gut. A disgorger, of the pattern familiar to river fishermen, may help, but I personally prefer a pair of long-bladed scissors, with which, after mercifully killing it first with a blow on the head, the fish is cut open and the hook removed without damage. Most of these flat-fish, and especially plaice, have a knack of doubling up in the water, thereby wofully deceiving the expectant angler in the matter of their weight. They are also, for the most part, smooth to handle, but in the plaice and dab there is a sharp spike in the ventral fin, which those with tender hands would do well to keep clear of.

The actual tackle best to use for these flat-fish is, I think, a light gut paternoster, on which two or three small hooks, also on single gut, are strung at intervals above the small pear-shaped lead. The line is allowed to run through the rod rings until the lead just rests on the bottom ; then the rod top is very slightly lowered, and the angler waits for the bite. Given stronger tackle, a sea-rod with large Nottingham reel, heavier lead, larger hooks, and either stout single salmon gut or else treble gut of finer strands, and the angler is equipped for the autumn boat-fishing for cod and whiting as practised at Deal and other resorts in the Channel.

It will be noticed that no practical hints have so far been given with regard to the capture of that king of British salt-water fishes, the bass, but the fact is, the majority of large bass are caught either drifting in estuaries, a mode of fishing to be presently described in some detail, or from piers and harbours, a style of fishing that belongs to the second part of these remarks. Where, however, there are sandy banks amongst the rocks, and lying in about ten or fifteen feet of not too clear water, large bass may sometimes be taken by the following not very sporting method.

The boat is moored fore and aft, so as to remain perfectly rigid and impart no movement to the line, and the line is coiled on the seat, so that it can be flung out without a check. If a rod is used, then sufficient is pulled off the reel. There is no lead, and the single hook, of the size previously shown for pollack, is embedded in a whole pilchard two or three days old. Bass like their dead food somewhat tasty, and not until the pilchard is sufficiently decomposed to be almost disgusting to the sensitive nose has it much chance of attracting a big bass. The manner in which the pilchard is put on the hook for this particular kind of fishing is not very easy to describe, but, briefly, the fish is first decapitated, the head being thrown out as ground bait, and, the hook having been passed twice through the body, a hitch of the gut is taken round the base of the tail-fin, the last-named being finally removed quite neatly with a sharp knife. The headless pilchard now hangs, so to speak, shoulders downwards, and it is heavy enough to carry out the line after being swung backwards and forwards once or twice. It is then thrown after the head, so as to fall on a sand "splat," where bass are known to feed after stormy weather (this method of fishing has little chance of success after a long spell of calm), and I have known my man pitch it with the greatest accuracy thirty or forty yards. The bait having been allowed to sink gently to the bottom, the line is slowly reeled in until it is almost tight, a little slack only being left in the boat. Under favourable conditions, *i.e.* with the boat properly moored and perfectly still water, this slack ought to lie quiet until a fish attacks the bait.

I have called this mode of fishing unsportsman-like, because there is a *dolce far niente* about it offensive to the keen sportsman. For now, look you, the fisherman may light his pipe or eat his luncheon, or even read his paper, so only he keeps an occasional weather eye on that slack line. Presently, if he is in luck, it will be seen to move ever so gently and unobtrusively away through the rod rings, or (with a hand-line) over the edge of the boat. And then he must relinquish his luncheon or his paper and give all his attention to the line. If using a rod, he should grasp it firmly, but without in the least disturbing the progress of the outgoing line, and he will do well, as an extra precaution—the slightest check would send the suspicious fish off in a panic, and he is not yet properly hooked—to point the rod in the direction in which the bass is taking the line, thus making friction practically impossible. The line will go more and more quickly, and at last there will be a run. Then, and not till then, let him smartly raise the

top of the rod and strike home. If he is using a
hand-line, he need not touch it at all until that last
run. Let him keep his hand poised in readiness
over it, so as to grasp and strike at the exact
moment. And let him, if the bass happens to be a
large one, as it usually is if caught in this way, play
it very gingerly indeed on a hand-line, for a heavy
bass on a hand-line with fine gear is about the most
difficult fish to play in our seas. The rod-fisher
has an enormous advantage, for the play of the top
joint takes a great deal of the strain off the line,
and he who uses the line only has to imitate this as
closely as possible with the give and take of his
hand and arm, which is no easy matter. Let the
boatman stand by with the net or gaff and make sure
of the fish as soon as possible ; a long struggle may
be tiring to the bass, but it is infinitely more so to
the tackle.

73—*LESSER WEEVER.*

74.—AFTER BASS.

CHAPTER XXIX

SEA-FISHING FROM BOATS:
BASS FISHING

By F. G. AFLALO

AND now we come to that calm-water fishing for
bass and others of the fish already named, to which
the attention of the seasick has been specially invited.

It has just been said that the bass likes high food.
So it does, when in the mood for carrion, and a decayed skate's liver is even more appealing than a
scented pilchard. Yet the bass is chiefly to be regarded as a predatory fish, and to see it feeding at
its best it should be watched from some high cliff,
dashing among the frightened shoals of sand-eels,

with its feathered allies shrieking just above the
surface. What a time of it these small fish must
have, to be sure ! The tenor wishes at intervals
that he were a bird, but not even Mr. Holbein
has ever wished himself a fish, though he could
hardly swim much better if he were. The bass,
then, pursues these small and delicate fishes not
only up and down the coast, but even into tidal
rivers, and there it may be sought by anglers whose
gorge would rise at the mere thought of embarking
in a boat in the open. The distance to which bass
thus engaged will penetrate into a country is not,
I think, satisfactorily determined. Its case is not
analogous to that of the salmon, which will ascend
as far as possible in search of pure water for its
precious ova. The bass could not, in all probability,
flourish in the head waters, nor does its search for
food take it as far. In the Arun, a river famous
in the annals of Sussex anglers, the bass are taken
above Arundel, where I have fished before now with
Slaughter—who, however, hardly justified his name
on those occasions—but not, I think, far above that
historic town. In the Teign, a bass river with which
I am very much better acquainted, the bass travel, it
is said, three parts of the way up to Newton, though
the larger fish at any rate have never, within the
memory of man, been taken on the rod any distance above the long footbridge, which can hardly
be more than half a mile from the bar. It is not
always easy to find these estuary bass, for there are
days on which they gather just off the mouth of the

river, and days on which they make their way up to
the bridge with all despatch and rarely look at a
bait until above the yacht moorings—I refer here
to the Teign estuary—or even up to the bridge itself.
They show considerable variation in size, my own
afore-mentioned fish of 11 lbs. 5 ozs. being from
all accounts the largest taken on the rod for the
past twenty years at any rate, if not indeed the
record for rod-caught fish in that river. That the
angler may always, however, expect something considerably heavier than this may be gathered from the
fact of a bass of close on double the weight, or 22
lbs., having been netted during the summer of 1902
in the river Tamar. This still leaves the record with
Devon, and indeed there are reasons why it should
be one of the finest counties for bass in the kingdom,
its many bar estuaries giving it a great advantage
over the more unbroken coast of Cornwall. Some
parts of Wales are also famous for bass, and Bar-
mouth was, at any rate till quite recently, as good
a goal as any for the angler specially bent on the
capture of this fish. Although I like a turn at all
manner of sea-fishing on occasion, even unto the
taking of flat-fish and gurnards, the coarse fishing of
the coast, I am rapidly coming to the conclusion
that there are only two sea-fish at home really worth
the attention of the scientific angler, and these are
the bass and grey mullet. Of the grey mullet,
more later when we find ourselves on *terra firma* ; of
the bass now, and that right speedily.

It has already been pointed out that these bass are

predatory, and that they follow the shoals of brit and small sand-eels some distance up our south-coast rivers. The bass come along in shoals also, the large and the small keeping to themselves with an exclusiveness that betokens caution on the part of the small. They usually begin to enter the river on each tide just as the ebb slacks off, and they run up until just on high water. On calm, hot days they may be seen playing at the surface, and the angler then follows them in his boat and picks a fish or two out of each shoal, just as he might in other circumstances pick a right and left out of each covey. There are days, however, when the fish do not, for some reason or other, show at the surface, and then he has to be guided by the gulls in attendance. And there are a few, a very few, days on which there are neither fish nor birds to indicate where he should cast his bait on the secretive waters ; and on such days I have sometimes taken large fish.

The tackle and baits which I use for this bass fishing have incidentally been described. A 10-foot trout-rod, a bronze winch holding about sixty yards of fine dressed silk line, ten or twelve feet of strongest single salmon gut, and a hook of the size figured [1] (Fig. 22, p. 252) are the chief items. Sometimes no lead whatever is used, and at others a piece of lead-foil weighing an ounce or less improves matters. The single hook is attached to the end of the gut collar,

[1] I show a square hook here for the sake of variety, though the round bends have latterly given me greater satisfaction.

the gut collar to the line, and the lead is pinched
on the latter just above the join of the gut.   The
one and only bait is a living, nay a lively, sand-eel
caught from the adjacent sand-bar ; and mark well
that it must be a brown sand-eel and not a green
launce.   The launce and sand-eels keep company in
the wet-sand flats at the entrance to the river, and
there they are netted daily throughout the summer,
unless an extra run on salmon or mackerel gives the
men more profitable occupation elsewhere.   Sixpence
invested in lively sand-eels is sufficient for a morning's bait for two rods, and they must be at once
transferred in a bucket of sea water to a floating
bait-box or a courge.   The courge is a torpedo-
shaped basket of wicker, which is convenient for
towing astern of the boat.   It was introduced from
the Channel Islands, I believe, by the late J. C.
Wilcocks, and is now in general use in the south-
west.   The floating bait-box, which, at any rate
for river work where there is no rough water, I
prefer, is triangular or wedge-shaped, perforated
with numerous holes, and having a small opening
which is covered by a lid working on leather hinges.
A good plan is to keep the bulk of the bait in a box
of this kind, which is towed, not astern but alongside, and to have a bucketful of water in the boat,
into which a dozen baits are transferred from time
to time as wanted.   These are more easily got at
when the fish are biting well, and it is consequently
necessary to have a fresh bait every minute or two,
as getting the box out of the water and into the

boat is a somewhat long business, it being desirable
to let all the water drain out of it before bringing it
over the side. The method of putting the sand-eel
on the hook has already been described. The hook
is passed through the lower lip, care being taken to
injure the delicate fish as little as possible, and the
point is then caught in the skin of the throat. This
is found to be the best way of keeping the bait lively
for the longest possible time, for, properly put on
the hook, it can swim and breathe without hindrance,
neither the fins nor gills being disturbed by the hook.
All being ready, the boat is rowed quietly and without fuss to a point below where the fish are known,
or thought, to be feeding, and, if the tide is at more
than one-third flood, the stern is brought round so as
to point upstream, and the boat is allowed to drift
in this fashion over the fish. The bait is lowered
quietly into the water, and line is paid out foot by
foot off the reel until the bait may be working forty
or fifty yards from the boat, the latter being prevented from overtaking the hook by gentle paddling.
I hope this is quite clear. The angler and the boatman both face upstream, the former sitting in the
stern-thwart with his back to the boatman in the
bow. During spring tides there is generally a deal
of green weed in the river, mostly out of the salmon
nets, and at such times it may be necessary to examine
the bait every few moments, as the least particle
of weed on it is sufficient to prevent the fish from
biting. It does not add to the pleasure of fishing
to reel in thirty or more yards of line at intervals

75.—GETTING TO WORK.

76.—BASS CAUGHT IN ALDE.

of two or three minutes to see whether the bait
is free of weed, especially when, as sometimes
happens, the precaution is repeatedly found to
have been unnecessary. It does not add to the
pleasure of fishing ; but it pays in the long run, for
there could be nothing more aggravating than to
reel in after a drift over the entire ground, a matter
of five or ten minutes, only to find that there is
weed on the bait, and to think that it might perhaps have been there ever since starting that drift.
If the bass are large, there will be no mistake about
the bite, and no difficulty about striking and hooking the fish, for the simple reason that it hooks
itself. There is a sudden curve of the top joint, a
scream of the reel, and the fun has commenced.
Unless the angler knows his work, it is as likely as
not to end very soon as far as he is concerned, for
the first rush of a heavy bass is easily bungled by
the fisherman, and a lost cast will be the result of
any carelessness. The fish must be allowed to run,
always with the least possible check of the finger on
the rim of the reel, and the moment the fish stops
the line must be very gingerly wound in. If the
tackle is strong, as bass tackle must be, then the
rule is to keep a tight line on the fish from first to
last. If the gut is frayed, or the angler has any
other cause to distrust his tools, then a certain
licence must be allowed, though this is at best but
a risky game, and the bass is more likely than not
to get away. A good bass of 5 lbs. or over will
sometimes run out yards and yards of line half-a-

dozen times over without giving up the struggle, and even when apparently exhausted such a fish will break away from the very point of the gaff or ring of the landing-net and start away again up-stream. The increasing strength of the tide, and, in this particular river, the swift rush of the waters between the piles of the bridge are immeasurably in its favour, and it is not slow to avail itself of such natural aids, of which it shows an accurate know-ledge, that can only be explained on the basis of its having been in that river many times before. Care should be taken, when the fish is safely in the boat, not to cut the hands against its spinous fins, for these inflict extremely nasty wounds. The smaller bass bite at times much more ravenously than the heavy fish, and they are also considerably more diffi-cult to hook, for they want quick striking at the moment of the bite. The bite itself is moreover so niggling that the angler is apt to mistake weed for fish. Once hooked, these little bass, which may run two, three, or five to the pound, give absolutely no sport, though for their size they fight gamely.

Such is bass fishing in the river, and it is about the most delightful form of salt-water fishing that I know. There is another mode of bass fishing in rivers which I have practised, with very little success, in the Arun, just above Arundel. In it the boat is moored near the reeds, and live-bait tackle with float is used, as for pike, the bait being a live roach or dace. Very large bass are occasion-

ally—very occasionally, I fancy—taken in this way,
but the angler must be prepared for many days on
which " man never is, but always to be, blest " !

When, as sometimes happens, the Devon bass
are sighted, not in the river, but just outside the
bar, the same bait and tackle are used as in the river
itself, only the boat has to be slowly rowed in circles
over the rocks. As the water is, just after low tide,
not more than six or eight feet deep, and as the
rocks are overgrown with waving " bootlace " weed,
the hook very often gets hung up, and breakages
are not uncommon. Nor do I recall a single instance during the past three years in which a bass
of more than 2 or 3 lbs. was taken outside the
river, though fifteen or twenty years ago, so resi-
dents relate, the last hundred yards just above the
bar used to be considered the only ground for
bass. Whether the large fish did not in those days
penetrate up as far as the bridge, or whether they were
there all the time and lay there undisturbed until
some genius located them, the chronicler sayeth not.
During the last five years or so, the " bridge swim "
has been the fashion, and I never wish for better
fun than it gives on favourable days. It must in
reason be admitted that these are wonderfully few.
Early morning is the best time, and I have often
been after these bass as early as four in the morning.
Both the large fish already mentioned in these pages
were taken before seven in the morning, and only
once do I remember a really good fish—I think it
weighed 9¼ lbs.—being taken in the middle of the

day. Narrow as is the river just below the bridge
—there is an immense mud bank in the centre,
where the natives are for ever digging the locally
appreciated cockle—there is ample room for half-a-
dozen boats or even more to fish for bass in company, if only they all drift in the right way up the
deep water channel. When, however, the man or
the boatman is wholly ignorant of the business—if
I named three local boat-owners who understand
bass fishing, I should exhaust the list, but I do not
wish to incur an action for libel, so the reader must
segregate for himself the sheep from the goats—
trouble is bound to ensue. As soon as another boat
commences moving backwards and forwards across
the river, and trailing the bait instead of paying it
out in front, lines are sure to foul. It is no good
haranguing the offender. I tried it once one summer, when my friends, Mr. Cyril Maude and "the
Doctor," were fishing with me, and this was the
result :—

Irate Angler. Would you mind keeping off my
line? (I do not, writing from memory, insist on
this as an accurate verbatim report, but the senti-
ment is the same.)

Insulted Visitor. Hare you speakin' to me?

I. A. I ham !

I. V. Look 'ere; is this (here followed two
words, which I take to be dialect for weedy and
swift-flowing) river yours, or may I fish here too ?

After which the Irate Angler maintained a freez-
ing silence. He knew that argument was useless

77.—*BASS IN THE HARBOUR.*

78.—IDLING.

with a person who could describe such footling as
"fishing," and, as there were ladies in other boats
in the neighbourhood, he also thought it better to
apply the closure, for

"Words, like Nature, half reveal
And half conceal the soul within ; "

and it seemed, judging from the sample revealed,
that the remainder of that beautiful soul would be
better for concealment.

Irritating episodes of this sort are, however, the
exception, and are in any case confined to the end-
July and August holiday season, which brings weird
wildfowl from the great and busy centres inland.
And there is, thank goodness, plenty of time to
catch bass before they come, and occasionally, in a
spell of Indian summer, after they are departed, un-
regretted by all save those who have given them
houseroom.

There is another kind of calm-water fishing in
boats in the latter part of the year, when whiting
and codling find their way into many rivers, notably
on our east coast. The Essex Blackwater and
Crouch, even for that matter the Thames at
Leigh, the river at Aldeburgh, and several others,
are the yearly playground of many anglers who like
to catch sea-fish in still water. A light gut paternoster, and either mussels, lugworms, or soft crab
for bait, are best for this fishing. The great difficulty is to hit off the tide. I remember once *not*
hitting off the tide at Maldon, on the Blackwater.

Everything had been arranged by telegram; Handley's yacht, well known to anglers in that part of the world, was in readiness, and I went down by the appointed train. Something went wrong, however, with the tides. Whether they were not as they should have been, or whether, as seems more probable, I had miscalculated the whole programme, I forget for the moment, but the result was disastrous. I write from memory, but I vaguely remember spending just twenty-four hours away from home, and fishing for about forty minutes, the tide being too swift before and after that time to admit of fishing at all. And during the forty minutes we caught only two or three midgets of fish, bullheads for the most part, if I remember right, and nothing worth taking away. That was an exceptionally unfortunate outing, however, and I have in other days enjoyed very brisk sport with these Essex whiting and codling on bright winter mornings, with the moon just giving place to a little less pale December sun. Nowadays, however, give me the warm summer fishing. When September has yielded its last bass, and when in the early days of October one has had a day or two with the inshore whiting and the late mackerel, with perhaps a chance cod or dory in the boat's well, then let the rod, for my part, be laid by in a dry, warm corner, and let the guns come out during play hours. Sitting wet and shivering in an open boat during the last two months of the year is to my mind the least satisfactory of sport. If I were bent on winter sea-fishing, which I am not, I would rather fish from shore or pier, where at any rate a man can walk up and down and make his blood spin faster when the fish hold aloof and he has time to realise how much more comfortable he would be beside his fire. I am aware that enthusiasts do manage to enjoy boat-fishing at Deal and elsewhere on the coldest or shortest day of the year, and more power to their elbow, but—"for me, No," as the Frenchman said when offered jugged hare.

CHAPTER XXX

SEA-FISHING FROM BOATS:
GENERAL REMARKS

By F. G. Aflalo

THIS, then, concludes what I have to say about
fishing from boats, but I do not want to take leave
of the subject without a few words of caution on
the subject of general procedure and behaviour in
such fishing. In the first place, I think it would
be as well if, without being in the least nervous,
every one who fishes from boats were made to realise
that any carelessness on his (or *her*) part may
jeopardise not alone the life of the culprit, but
also of the rest of the party, particularly of the
unfortunate boatman, who, besides being as a rule

79.—A GOOD ONE ON

80.— STRIKING.

hampered by heavy clothes the reverse of helpful to any one suddenly projected into the water, is in ninety-nine cases out of every hundred quite ignorant of the art of swimming. It is a well-known fact, and one which I have confirmed by directly questioning dozens of men so placed, that those who cannot swim have no fear of drowning. It is the old story of ignorance and bliss, the same blessed indifference as causes the newcomer to disdain the tropical sun or the Arctic cold, and to venture abroad in supreme disregard of the special clothing and other precautions adopted by those long resident in the place. The non-swimmer never realises the danger of collapse, as he might had he once fought with a strong current, as most swimmers have done in their time; and this is within certain limits a good thing, else half the best fishermen on the coast could never be induced to go afloat, and the younger generation, most of whom are able to swim, would never have a chance of learning by direct instruction the arts by which their fathers and grandfathers have earned their livelihood time out of mind. At the same time, it is only right to remember how these men are situated, and to be extra careful not to put their lives| in any danger. A sailing-boat may be put in danger through the vanity of an amateur who insists on retaining the helm in a squall and on a coast with which he is unfamiliar. A rowing-boat, or at any rate its occupants, may be put in still greater danger through any one standing up in it.

Ladies—I shiver at my own temerity, but it must be said—are the most untiring offenders in this respect. As sure as a steamer passes so near as to rock the boat with the wash from her paddles, so, just at the worst moment, a lady in the boat will stand up. The precise object of this interesting demonstration I have never been able to fathom. Is it perhaps a sudden desire to protest against the disturbance? Does it rather rest on some vague, half-conscious animal instinct to get out of the boat and seek safety elsewhere? I know not. The fact remains that those divine beings, whom we all cherish, do stand up in boats just as surely as they hop backwards and forwards in suicidal uncertainty when crossing Oxford Circus in heavy traffic.

Another thing to be very careful of in a boat is that nothing is so placed that any one may slip on it. A boat is not the place to slip in. The worst case of this that I know is when men are shooting seals or porpoises, or maybe cormorants, with rifles, and the empty brass cartridge cases are thrown in the bottom of the boat instead of overboard. I have seen many a disagreeable fall in this way, and on one occasion—it was out in Australia—a man nearly pitched overboard. When you pitch overboard in Australia you may have the quaint luck to pitch into the open jaws of an appreciative shark. Round objects, such as cartridges, thole pins, leaden bullets, and so on, are obviously more dangerous in such situations than others, but there is, or should be, a place for everything in

a boat as well as out of it, and in that place let it be
kept. For a similar reason no slippery piece of
bait or fish should be left in spots where people
are likely to step on them. Moreover, a little
cleanliness in the boat is immensely conducive to
the general comfort, particularly when there is any
one whose stomach easily rebels.

With regard to the correct methods of launching
and beaching and anchoring small boats, these
matters are much better learnt on the spot. In
the absence of skilled assistance, a little presence
of mind and common-sense will go a great way.
It will be apparent that to throw the whole weight
in the bow of the boat when launching will not
only make the work much more difficult, but will
also make the risk of an upset at the start considerably greater. In beaching, too, it is advisable in
most cases to back the boat in stern first, and when
there is a swell or lop care must be taken to come
in just behind a wave and not just in front of it.
As to anchoring, this presents no difficulty as a rule
with quite small boats, provided always that the
anchor is efficient and the rope long enough. To
put a heavy sailing-boat on a particular rock in
twenty or thirty fathoms of water requires a good
deal more practice, but one always takes a professional fisherman on such occasions, and he knows
all about tatchings and splices and allowance for
wind and tide. The anchor may, under certain
conditions, be dropped ten or fifteen yards from
the spot where the hooks should lie, but the wind

and tide do the rest. In anchoring the boat on the
sand, an anchor of the orthodox pattern will be
requisite, but for fishing on the rocks a large square
stone, or "killick," is generally sufficient. I have
sometimes managed quite well with the stone on
the sand, but it is not so generally useful in that
place as an anchor. In Cornwall, indeed, the
peculiar form of anchor known as a "grapnel"
(locally pronounced "graper") is used under all
conditions, and a nice business it sometimes is to
haul it clear of the rocks. A "tatching" is made,
which has the effect of disengaging it wrong way
up, but sometimes, in spite even of this precaution,
it is impossible to get it free at high water. The
only plan is then to attach a cork buoy, with your
initials cut or burnt deeply in, by a long line, and
seek the anchor again at the next convenient low
tide, taking the bearings of its position very carefully to facilitate picking it up again. When doing
the same thing at low water, it is important to
attach the buoy by a very long line, else it will be
carried under and lost to sight in the deeper water
at the flood. It is at flood-tide that submerged
lobster-pots or trammels, with their hidden corks
and ropes, are so fatal to the amateur's tackle,
particularly when he is whiffing for pollack or
mackerel and thus dragging his hooks through the
water. When the tide is low and slack, the tell-
tale corks are easily seen, and a very little care
should suffice to steer the lines clear of the obstacle.
When, however, all indication is hidden, collision

may easily result. The only plan is to let out slack
line, from either the rod reel or winder of the hand-
line, and to back the boat on to the trammel or pot
in which the hooks are fast. Even then, it may be
impossible to recover all the gear, but something
at any rate may be saved. It would be impossible
to haul a large trammel to free the hook, as that
is a laborious job involving the joint labours of
several men used to the work. The lobster-pot,
however, could easily be hauled and lowered again
after the hook had been recovered. It would probably be found not in the pot itself, but in the rope
some way below the surface. How far the fisherman is justified in disturbing a pot in which his
hook is fast is a question in ethics which I am not
called upon to decide, since in such a matter every
one will settle for himself. Personally, I should
feel justified in disturbing the pot to recover my
hook if I also thought it worth while. Hauling
a lobster-pot in deep water and a strong tide is,
however, a pastime which may appeal to some, but
not to me, and I had rather lose a dozen hooks than
go to so much trouble.

Those who own small yachts, by the way, might
do worse than invest in a correspondingly small
trammel. The trammel is virtually a net wall,
standing about six feet high, and doing its work in
the dark. More explicitly, it consists of three upright nets, the two outer nets being short, stretched
tight between the ropes, and having a large mesh
through which the fish can pass, the middle net

being much longer, left slack between the others, and having a mesh so small that it arrests the fishes. When a fish swims against the outer net, on either side, it passes easily through the large mesh, and then, still swimming on, goes through the large mesh of the opposite outer net, but with the small-meshed, loose middle net caught over its head and shoulders. This frightens it into darting forward to escape, and that seals its fate, for it is now in a net bag, like any bolted rabbit, and the harder it struggles the tighter it draws the fatal meshes. A small trammel, from fifteen to twenty fathoms, is sufficient for the amateur to amuse himself and supply his yacht with, and Hearder, of Plymouth, would probably supply one of that length for between four and five sovereigns. The trammel is stretched between two lines with lead below and a buoy above, and a series of leads on the lower edge and of corks on the upper serve to keep it in its upright position. It is set from the yacht's dinghey, and the process involves only a little care to pay it out clear and without fouling. On the lee-side of a reef of rocks and parallel with the tide is a likely situation, and it may be set at sunset and taken up before turning-in. Some yachtsmen leave it out close to the yacht all night, but I never found this answer, as, unless one thoroughly knew the ground to an extent very uncommon in the wandering yachtsman, the net either got fouled at the change of tide or else full of small crabs, which were not slow to help themselves to the red mullet, dory, bass, or other good fish helpless to defend themselves against even the most puny aggressor.

A small trawl is also kept aboard some yachts, and one of very manageable dimensions for amateur purposes could be purchased for about five or six sovereigns, with all gear complete. As, however, I have been a constant advocate of increased restrictions on this amateur trawling, which, in the shallow inshore waters, does more damage in proportion to its effective strength than the serious trawling on the outer grounds, and as, moreover, there is nothing sporting in the wholesale greed of this sweeping net, I think it more consistent to refrain from giving any practical hints as to the working of an engine already far too popular. Nor do I care about suggesting the greater popularising of the seine, or sean, though this is at any rate generally "shot" round a well-located shoal of some round fish, like the bass, the mullet, or the mackerel, and does less harm than the trawl (though quite enough, for all that) to the flat-fish. A small sean, for the purpose of amusement, would cost five or six sovereigns, and there is this to distinguish it from the trawl or trammel, that it gives healthful exercise. Those who work it must not mind a wetting even to the waist, and there is an amount of hard pulling that must brace the muscles to a wonderful extent. The sean is "shot" with the aid of a boat in a semicircle, the one end of the rope being left with a man on the beach, and the other brought round in a semicircular sweep by the boat to another point on the beach some distance higher up. The two ends are then hauled close together, and all manner of fish are taken in the small-meshed bunt. Among the fish that I have seen caught in this way are not only those named above, but also sand-eels and launce, monk-fish and small sharks, turbot, soles, and plaice, dory, shad, garfish, and in fact all those fish which haunt an open shore in shallow water.

A word or two on the cost of sea-tackle may not perhaps be out of place in bringing this section to a close, but it is not convenient to go into the subject in much detail, for a comprehensive account from the standpoint of every grade of income would occupy more than the available space.

Tackle specially made for sea-fishing in the old style is not, as a rule, costly. The made-up lines with special fittings work out somewhat higher than might seem necessary, but even these rarely cost more than six or seven shillings complete. On the other hand, if the fisherman makes up his own lines from the raw material, or rather from the manufactured parts, as he certainly should do, he need not spend the half of what these mounted lines would cost him. He can get fifteen or twenty fathoms of tanned line for two or three shillings, and the gut, lead, and hooks together need not cost as much again. The usual pattern of stout sea-rod costs from half a guinea to a guinea or a little more, and the Nottingham winch suitable for sea-fishing, most costly item of all, may run into thirty or forty shillings.

81.—*EXPECTATION.*

82.—THE ENTHUSIAST.

Personally, I spend more on the rod and less on the reel. A sea-trout rod, costing a couple of guineas, is balanced by a small bronze check winch at ten or twelve shillings, and this combination suits admirably for the heaviest bass, as also for moderate-sized pollack, for mackerel, or for mullet. The artificial baits used in sea-fishing are far cheaper than those used by the pike or salmon fisher. The "flies" for pollack, bass, or mackerel only cost twopence or threepence each, and the indiarubber baits so extensively used come to little more. Natural baits, particularly living sand-eels, may run into a considerable sum during the season, but so, on the other hand, do live baits for pike. Boat hire is certainly more costly as a rule than in fresh water, but even then it need not alarm, and members of the British Sea Anglers' Society get preferential rates at many ports.

A FLYING FISH

	s.	d.
The beft plaice	0	1½
A dozen of beft foles	0	3
Beft frefh mulvil, i. e. Molva, either cod or ling	0	3
Beft hadock	0	2
Beft barkey	0	4
Beft mullet	0	2
Beft dorac, *John Doree?*	0	5
Beft conger	1	0
Beft turbot	0	6
Beft bran, fard, and betule	0	3
Beft mackrel, in *Lent*	0	1
And out of *Lent*	0	0½
Beft gurnard	0	1
Beft frefh merlings, i. e. *Merlangi*, whitings, four for	0	1
Beft powdered ditto, 12 for	0	1
Beft pickled herrings, twenty	0	1

This fhews that the invention of pickling was before the time, of *William Benkelen*, who died in 1397. See *Brit. Zool.* iii. article *Herring*.

	s.	d.
Beft frefh ditto, before *Michaelmas*, fix for	0	1
Ditto, after *Michaelmas*, twelve for	0	1
Beft *Thames*, or *Severn* lamprey	0	4
Beft frefh oyfters, a gallon for	0	2
A piece of rumb, grofs and fat, I fufpect *Holibut*, which is ufually fold in pieces, at	0	4
Beft fea-hog, i. e. porpeffe	6	8
Beft eels, a ftrike, or ½ hundred	0	2
Beft lampreys, in winter, the hundred	0	8
Ditto, at other times	0	6

Thefe, by their cheapnefs, muft have been the little lampreys now ufed for bait.

But we alfo imported lampreys from *Nantes*: the firft which came

in

CHAPTER XXXI

Section II

SEA-FISHING FROM FIXED POSITIONS

By F. G. Aflalo

A BOAT may, of course, be to all intents and purposes a fixed position, provided the boat be sufficiently large and the water sufficiently smooth. I have fished from a 6000 - ton steamer in an Australian estuary, or, again, when hung up in the Suez Canal, and there was no more movement than if I had been conducting operations

from the Admiralty Pier, Dover, the pebbly fore-
shore near Aldeburgh, or any one of my favourite
rocky headlands down in the west country. In the
ordinary way, however, the above distinction is one
with which few will quarrel, and the very rare occasions on which the sea-angler at home is able to
demonstrate the absolute immobility of his boat
are rather evidence of his well-behaved stomach
than of the truth of his proposition.

Now, each form has its advantages and its drawbacks. The advantages of the boat are obvious,
for it takes the angler away from the shallow and
disturbed water inshore to the haunts of the big
fish; and if they are not feeding on one ground, it
quickly transports him to another, till he comes in
luck's way. The pier-fisher or beach-fisher has to
wait till luck comes his way. He cannot seek it.
The Moors, who are artists in the finer interpreta-
tions of leisure, do some of their shooting this way.
A Moor will load his long-barrelled flintlock gun,
and he will then sit with it on a dry and stony hill-
side for an hour or for six, as may be necessary,
until some bird flies overhead or perhaps a hare goes
lolloping along in front. Then he fires, and generally misses. Then he loads again, and this time,
after another interval, he may bring down a hawk
or a hoopoe. After all, the boat-fisher, save when
he is whiffing for mackerel or pollack, also sits still,
but he at any rate sits him in the highway of the
fishes, and when he has sat long enough in one spot
without getting a bite, he fetches up his anchor,

sets his sail, and proceeds to sit in another. The
drawbacks of the boat are also sufficiently patent:
danger, discomfort, and expense may all in greater
or less degree rule it out of court. On the other
hand, sea-fishing from piers and beaches is not
without its advantages, though some of these will
be more obvious to the beginner than others. What
will strike every one, even without any special knowledge of sea-fishing, is that the pier or beach gives
immunity from sea-sickness; that it may be fished
from in all weathers; and that it costs little or
nothing, since the small fees charged for fishing
from some piers with a high reputation, deserved
or otherwise, for fishing can in no way compare with
the considerable cost of boats, particularly when it
is necessary to hire the larger sailing-boats, with
two hands, in order to reach the outer fishing
grounds. These three considerations, then, in
favour of fishing from fixed positions, as I have
called them, will occur to all. Less obvious to those
with no knowledge of the sport is the manner in
which such positions bring the angler within reach
of really sporting fish. There are fishes which, like
the bass, the pollack, and the grey mullet, frequent
the neighbourhood of piers at one season or another
for the sake of the food, probably the small crustaceans that harbour in the seaweed on the piles,
and also perhaps for shelter. In certain conditions,
too, of wind and tide, the bass in summer, and the
cod and whiting in winter seek their food just
behind the surf of the breaking waves, for which

reason there is at such times a better chance of catching them from a rocky headland or sandy beach than there would be if fishing in a boat, since the boat could not venture sufficiently close to the broken water to bring the angler within reach of the fish. The angler, moreover, who has access to an open sandy coast, but not to a boat of any kind, may catch fish by one or two special methods, which, though they may not in every case come up to the highest standard of sport, are yet very profitable at times, and these will be described after some reference has been made to the more regular ways of fishing.

Without further preamble, then, as to the ethics of fishing from the shore or from piers, I will now endeavour to give some hints whereby such of the afore-mentioned methods of fishing as are practicable in these situations may be adapted to the altered conditions.

In his usual ingenious style, my friend, " John Bickerdyke," has in his Badminton volume on " Sea-Fishing " traced an imaginary evolution of the rod on a rocky coast, primitive man having repeatedly torn his line against the shell-edged rocks until the happy thought came to him to cut an ash sapling, and thus haul fish and line clear of these obstacles. In the ordinary course, indeed, the rod, generally with float tackle, may be regarded as the correct gear for fishing from the rocks, while the hand-line is more appropriate to a sandy beach, though, as will presently be shown, a kind of rod-

arrangement is sometimes used to enable the fishermen to fling it sufficiently far. Touching this long
casting, it is to be remarked that long casting does
not always mean more fish. There are much advertised tournaments of fly-casting and bait-casting,
and on such occasions it is no doubt a fine thing to
cast farther than your neighbour. In actual fishing, however, the man who casts far often throws
his baits right over the heads of the fish, and pitches
them out of their reach. If I use float tackle from
a pier or from rocks, I always search every foot of
water up to the foot of the one or of the other.
Thus, if the tide is going out, I drop in the float
close to the rocks or close alongside the pier, and
let the falling tide carry it gradually out twenty or
thirty yards, pulling line off the reel as required. If,
on the other hand, the tide is rising, I pitch the
float twenty or thirty yards—this can be done with
a long rod and a little practice—and let the water
bring it in to my feet, not removing it for another
cast until it is touching the rocks or the pier, as the
case may be. When, in autumn, numbers of small
pollack—up to a couple of pounds in weight—as-
semble under Teignmouth pier, they are to be seen
at low water swimming round and round among the
posts. Catching them in such circumstances on a
trout-rod is no easy matter, for one has to keep the
frantic fish, when hooked, clear of the ironwork.
Yet to fish outside would be to catch nothing. The
fish feed only right under the pier. The same may
be said of bass or grey mullet when caught along-

side of quays. These fish are alike in their habit of routing with their noses among the slimy woodwork of many of our docks, and the float must be dropped noiselessly so that the baits dangle close to the walls, and are there sucked by the prowling fish as if from the wood or iron itself. If the float were cast out into the stream or harbour a dozen feet from the wall, the bait might lie there unnoticed throughout the day.

336

FISH BROUGHT TO MARKET

s. d.

in was fold for not lefs than - - 1 4
A month after, at - 0 8
Beft freſh falmon, from Cbriſtmas to Eaſter, for - - 5 0
Ditto, after ditto - 3 0
Beft fmelts, the hundred 0 1
Beft roche, in fummer 0 1

s. d.

Beft Lucy, or pike, at · 6 8
By the very high price of the pike, it is very probable that this fiſh had not yet been introduced into our ponds, but was imported at this period as a luxury, pickled, or fome way preferved.

AMONG thefe fiſh, let me obferve, that the conger is, at prefent, never admitted to any good table; and to fpeak of ferving up a porpeffe whole, or in part, would fet your guefts a ftaring. Yet, fuch is the difference of tafte, both thefe fiſhes were in high efteem. King Richard's mafter cooks have left a moft excellent receipt for Congur in Sawfe*; and as for the other great fiſh, it was either eaten roafted, or falted, or in broth; or furmente with porpeffe †. The learned Doctor Caius even tells us the proper fauce, and fays, that it ſhould be the fame with that for a Dolpbin ‡; another diſh unheard of in our days. From the great price the Lucy or pike bore ‖, one may reafonably fufpect that it was at that time an exotic fiſh, and brought over at a vaſt expence.

I CONFESS myfelf unacquainted with the words Barkey, Bran, and Betule: Sard was probably the Sardine or Pilchard: I am equally at a lofs about Croplings, and Rumb: but the pickled Ba-

* Forms of Cury, 52.   † 54, 39, 56.
‡ Caii opufcula, 116.   ‖ Britiſh Zoology, iii. 320.

lenes

CHAPTER XXXII

SEA-FISHING FROM FIXED POSITIONS:
FISHING FROM ROCKS

By F. G. Aflalo

The most extraordinary rock-fishing—we will for
convenience take our "fixed positions" in this order:
rocky shores, sandy shores, and piers—that I ever
took part in was on the coast of Australia. I did
not take a leading part, it is true, for a couple of
experiences of those giddy clambers up goat tracks,

83.—*THROWING FROM THE ROCKS—BACK. P.T.O.*

84.—*THROWING FROM THE ROCKS—FORWARD.*

with a cauldron of surf and perhaps a happy family
of sharks in readiness a hundred feet below, held no
attraction for a sporting taste singularly deficient in
imagination. Born Australians run up and down
these ledges in the cliffs with an indifference to
danger that would do credit to a rock-rabbit; but I
am neither a born Australian nor a rock-rabbit, and
I stoutly declined to have any further traffic with
such unholy recreation. There is a certain amount
of rock-fishing, though in somewhat less dangerous
circumstances, since the sharks at any rate are
eliminated from the possibilities of disaster, on the
east coast of Scotland in the neighbourhood of
Aberdeen. Pollack and coal fish are taken in the
coves and bays of the coast between Aberdeen and
Stonehaven; and the fishermen use long rods and
fine tackle, baiting their hooks with the inside of
shore crabs or with large mussels.

Fishing from the rocks is in wide vogue throughout the Mediterranean, and those who have in great
steamers called at the different ports, at Gibraltar,
at Marseilles, at Leghorn, at Naples, at Palermo,
must have noticed at almost all of these immense
bamboo rods projecting from favourite fishing spots
on the rocks. Biarritz is another famous place for
the use of these long rods from the rocks, though
they will more often be seen in clusters on the jetties
on either side of the Port aux Pêcheurs. Wherever
the face of the rock slopes outwards, a long rod, one
of fifteen or twenty feet, is clearly essential to haul
the fish clear of the rock itself. Where, on the

other hand, as rarely happens, the rock falls sheer into deep water, like the side of a wall, then a short rod or even a hand-line would meet the requirements of the situation.

Float tackle is *par excellence* the most killing manner of fishing from the rocks, or for the matter of that from piers and harbours, particularly in cases where the bottom is also rocky and therefore likely to get foul of leads. Those who are already familiar with the principles of float-fishing in lake or river need only be told that an extra strong set of tackle is wanted in salt water, and the float, though made as sensitive as possible by accurate shotting of the line beneath it, must not dance and bob to every little ripple on the surface of the sea. A good thick pike-float answers the purpose admirably, and some arrangement whereby it can easily be shifted up or down the line is essential, as in some places the depth alters very rapidly, and it is necessary to fish with great accuracy at a certain distance from the bottom. Although, as already suggested, the sensitiveness of the float adds considerably to the angler's enjoyment, it must be admitted that the three fish chiefly caught by this means alongside rocks—bass, pollack, and mackerel—do not, as a rule, take the bait with the half-hearted appetite of wary carp. With them, on the contrary, it is all or nothing; a quick rush, and the float disappears in a swirl of water, and the line tightens with a twang. In fishing for grey mullet, on the other hand, which will be described on a later page in connection with pier-fishing, the biting may on occasion be so delicate that a light quill float, such as that used for Thames roach, may give the best results and the fewest misses.

As some of the best fishing close to a rocky shore is to be had in the twilight, after the sun is down in the west, it is a good plan to paint the top of the float with a dash of French white, or else to stick a very small white feather in the cap by which the float is made fast to the line. The eye soon accustoms itself to the small white spot, and by this means it is enabled to follow without difficulty the slightest movement on the part of the float long after the failing light would, without some such precaution, have rendered this impossible to the ordinary eyesight. Where the water runs to a considerable depth—*i.e.* eight or ten fathoms—close up to the rocks, a somewhat exceptional condition, and where the fish are feeding not far from the bottom, float tackle is not always effective. The great length of line intervening between the float and the hook hampers the movements of the former, and the biting of the fish is not always communicated to the float and thence to the angler's eye with sufficient promptness to give time for the necessary stroke to drive the hook home.

In such a case the paternoster may prove the more useful piece of tackle, and it is well to remember that the paternoster may be made up with any degree of either strength or fineness, from the delicate single-gut contrivance, with its little green pear of lead, used by perch fishers on Thames locks, to the stout treble-gut arrangements with their bars of brass, or whalebone, or cane, sold for sea-fishing in deep water and among big fish. A compromise between these two will, as a rule, be found the best tackle in ordinary fishing from the rocks. The water is not, as a rule, very deep; it is often very clear; and the fish caught seldom weigh much over 3 or 4 lbs., save when an exceptionally large pollack or bass, or maybe a conger eel, that has lost its way home, moves off with the bait with that slow but sure progress so certainly indicative of a heavy fish at the business end of the line. When conger fishing at night, by the way, stout tackle may be used anywhere from the rocks, as one is always liable to hook an immense fish even close to the shore. A paternoster of strong single gut should be sufficiently strong for ordinary bass or pollack fishing from the rocks, and it is as well to attach the lead by a frayed loop of line. When, as may some-times happen, the lead catches fast in the rocks on the bottom, it may be sacrificed, and the entire line, hooks and all, recovered, after which the addition of a spare lead enables the angler to resume fishing with very little loss of either time or tackle. Only practice will tell the angler just when he should strike when using a paternoster. There is no tell-tale float to guide him in choosing the right moment. As a general rule—one, however, to which actual practice furnishes many exceptions—the first " nig-gling " bite of the fish should be the signal for him to lower the top of his rod ever so slightly, and if,

as should happen, the fish is encouraged by this con-
cession to take the bait in earnest, he may then strike
as if he meant it and reel in. The object of the
paternoster being to offer the baits at different
depths, it is a good plan, unless the angler is quite
certain of the right bait for that locality, or unless,
as may be the case, he has only one kind of bait at
his disposal, to use two or even three baits, one on
each hook, until he is able to form some opinion
as to which the fish are taking at the time in preference to the rest. There is no rule, but, speaking
roughly, if fishing from a headland for bass, one
might bait the top hook with a living sand-eel,
hooked through the upper lip, the middle hook with
a strip of squid, and the bottom hook of all with
either a lump of ray's liver, a piece of fresh herring,
a green crab, or a couple of mussels. If none of
these, each in its way being a most killing bait for
bass, produced any result after a reasonable trial, it
might then not unfairly be assumed that the bass
had migrated elsewhere. Although the specific
object of the paternoster is undoubtedly to search
different depths, it may also, when used from the
shore, be used in trying different spots in the hori-
zontal plane, and this is done by casting it carefully
out and using it at an obtuse angle with the rod
instead of letting it hang vertically. By gradually
reeling in line, provided due care be taken not to
get the lead foul of a rocky bottom, it is surprising
how much water may be searched in this way. When
the same, or different, fish are, as sometimes happens,

feeding well at different depths, but rather too near the surface for the ordinary paternoster (in which the lead is not more than a foot at most from the lowermost hook) to be of use, a killing combination may be made of paternoster and float tackle by simply removing the heavier lead and substituting a small bullet, just sufficient to " cock " the float. Needless to say, this, or any other form of float tackle, is useful only in calm weather, as any considerable disturbance of the water is fatal to the sensitive working of the float.

Where there is a sandy bottom immediately within the rock-angler's reach, a leger-tackle for flat-fish or whiting will perhaps be found to answer best, but as the principle and management of this tackle will be fully described when reference is made to fishing from sandy beaches, it is not necessary to go into the details here.

Save when fishing from very high rocks, such as those resorted to by my Australian friends when tired of life and anxious to die fishing, a rod should always be used by the rock-fisher, for here, if anywhere, is its legitimate sphere of usefulness. Certainly, the life of the rod would be shortened by using it fifty feet or so above the water, but, unless it be near Aberdeen, where I have not yet had the pleasure of fishing, there are few spots on our coasts where so great an altitude is necessary. If, however, some unusual opportunity should occur of catching large fish from the upper ledge of a lighthouse, or some such position, let the fisherman

85.—SHOVING OFF.

86.—ANGLING FROM THE ROCKS

by all means content himself with a hand-line, and haul his fish into safety as soon as possible without any attempt at playing them. Such fishing must necessarily be directed chiefly towards the requirements of the pot, and sport is then at a discount.

While on the subject of rock-fishing, I may perhaps be pardoned if I add a word or two on the chief methods of taking such delicacies as prawns. These, though not perhaps coming very definitely under the rubric of sport, furnish a delicious article of food, and there is, if not actually sport, a very agreeable sensation in carefully hauling the prawn-pots, or examining the shovenet, while a little prawn fishing may be done in the intervals of more serious work.

Most rocky coasts furnish prawns, and if it is added that these are best taken during the spring tides, about three hours after low water, and in the deep pools that lie on the shady side of high rocks, little more need be said as to the when and where. There are two distinct ways of taking prawns Either they may be sought in the hand-net, or baited pots may be set for their capture. The choice is a matter of taste. Those who want to catch prawns and nothing more, and who moreover like the exercise and do not mind the immersion, often to the waist—for these rock pools are apt to be treacherous on a rising tide—will probably choose the hand-net. It has the advantage of being inexpensive, and five shillings or less should purchase one of the necessary mesh and strength. The handle should be short, and it is a great advantage, too often overlooked, if the frame on which the net is stretched has a square front instead of the more common rounded one. The reason for this preference is that the prawns have a way, particularly when their home is disturbed, of hugging the side of the rock, from which they have to be scooped by the skilful hand like flies from a wall, and it is impossible to brush the perpendicular side of the rock so close that none shall escape if the net be a round one. There is no great difficulty attaching to this manner of taking prawns beyond a little local knowledge as to the best times and places. Given this, if the prawn fisher bears in mind my simile of brushing flies off a wall, and, further, if he is always careful to work his net from below upwards, and not sideways, he should catch his score or two of fine prawns without fail. August and September are the best months; indeed on many parts of the coast (notably in Devon and Cornwall) these coveted crustaceans appear not to come so close inshore at any other period of the year.

The other method of prawning is more complicated, and consists in setting baited pots. These, with the necessary cork buoys and ropes, may cost about half a guinea apiece, more or less according to the make and material. They are of wire or cane, the latter being, I believe, much better, but also infinitely less portable and therefore unsuited to the requirements of the amateur unless he resides within easy reach of the sea or has his yacht or

other boat permanently on the shore. The only
other requisites for this prawn fishing are a long-
handled boat-hook, for lowering and recovering
the pots, and a few small gurnards, about three
to each pot, for bait. Gurnards, red or grey, are
the only bait that I know to be of much use for
prawns, though there are doubtless others. All
the commoner kinds of fish, however, such as
plaice, whiting, herring, &c., I have tried times
and again without result. An infinity of small
crabs they certainly attract, but of prawns ne'er a
one. One other bait, by the way, I recollect using
years ago, and that was ordinary shore crabs, such
as those just alluded to. The claws and legs were
removed, and a skewer was thrust through the body
from shoulder to shoulder. Half-a-dozen of these
transfixed in a row used to be considered, not without
reason, good enough bait for prawns. The pot being
baited, it is quietly and carefully lowered, by hitching
the boat-hook in the line, in a dark, deep pool, one
on which the sun does not fall direct—indeed, the
best catch of prawns will frequently be made between half-past five and half-past six on evenings
when the tide is at its highest about eight—and
there left. Three or four such pots may be lowered
in different pools, and the fisherman may then turn
his serious attention to any bass or pollack in the
neighbourhood, merely hauling the pots once every
ten minutes or so and transferring the prawns to a
bag. A lively prawn may now and again be dedi-

cated to the hook if float tackle is being used, and
it may score the heaviest pollack of all. The pots
are duly lowered again, and in this way a good dish
of prawns is sometimes secured without in any way
interfering in the other fishing. Quiet is essential to
success in prawning by either method. Prawns are
among the most shy dwellers in the rock pools,
and the least disturbance—and a two-legged ogre
suddenly invading their peaceful homes can hardly
be regarded as a trifle—is often sufficient to
send them scuttling away into deep crannies from
which it may be impossible to dislodge them. It
is advisable, when wading among the rocks for
prawns, to wear an old pair of boots, but these should
not be either buttoned or laced. It is not sufficient
to protect the sole of the foot only, as some do by
wearing sand shoes, for the sides of the pools, which
generally bristle with mussels, often give very nasty
cuts, and one cannot, in the excitement of prawning,
be sufficiently careful to have the ankles efficiently
protected. A cut is not, even if deep, generally
noticed while the limb is still immersed in the cold
water, but the loss of blood may be considerable,
and it occasionally happens, particularly if the blood
is a little out of order, that such a cut may have
long and nasty results, all of which risk may be
obviated by wearing old boots as suggested. It is
also very necessary, particularly if he whose soul
is set on prawns happens to be unable to swim, to
keep a continual eye on the rising of the waters.

87.—CLOSE INSHORE.

The rapidity with which, particularly during the second half of the flood—*i.e.* often the best time for prawning—the sea may come swirling round those rocks and cut off the careless and absorbed prawner from dry land, is amazing ; and every summer holiday season has its dismal chronicle of dreadful drowning accidents—last season was even above the average in its crop of fatalities—to warn, in vain, the inexperienced. It has been said above that about three hours after low water is the best time for catching prawns, but it should be added to this recommendation that much depends on the coast formation. On some parts of the coast, where long rocky causeways go jutting out from above high-water mark to below low-water mark, it may be possible to catch prawns from immediately after low water almost until the tide has done flowing. Where, on the other hand, the rocks do not reach as high as high-water line, it may be impossible to "fish" after half tide. The third hypothetical case, in which there are rocks near high-water mark but only sand beyond, is one in which prawning is practically out of the question, for these animals do not trouble themselves about rocky fastnesses which are uncovered to the light of day during two-thirds of the twenty-four hours.

There are other recreations for the rock-fisher, such as probing in dark crevices with an iron hook mounted in an ash handle for congers or lobsters, but these do not, perhaps, present sufficient difficulty

to make any detailed account necessary. One warning may, however, be uttered, and that is that no one
who is not tired of life should ever be induced, particularly when alone, to thrust his hand and arm into
a cleft on the rock, however tempting the dimly seen
form of a lobster or conger may look when just out
of reach of his ash handle and hook. It is often easier
to thrust the arm in than to withdraw it, particularly
if a large conger when hooked in this way suddenly
retreats, with an immense muscular effort, farther
into its cave, dragging with it the fisherman's arm
farther into the narrowing hole. Appalling cases
of death by drowning have been recorded from
this cause, the would-be captor being held a prisoner
until the waters slowly cut him off from help and
life—truly a dreadful ending.

It is impossible to give here a complete guide to
those portions of the coast at which the amateur
may find good fishing from the rocks, as distinguished from the generality of resorts where
there are reefs of rocks within reach of his boat.
The Scotch coast near Aberdeen and Stonehaven
is, as already mentioned, the home of rock-fishing
in this island, but the London angler may prefer
to go to the south-west coast, where, in Devon and
Cornwall, he may find plenty of spots at which
rock-fishing is often practicable. Near Hope's
Nose, for instance, in the neighbourhood of Babba-
combe and Torquay, as well as on the other side of
Torbay, just inside Berry Head, I have seen rod-

fishers enjoying some sort of sport. There are many
spots for this rock-fishing just west of Plymouth,
and it may be followed at almost every coast town
in Cornwall, though the best of the fishing is
unquestionably to be had from boats.

CHAPTER XXXIII

SEA-FISHING FROM FIXED POSITIONS: FISHING FROM SANDY SHORES

By F. G. AFLALO

FISHING from a sandy shore is practised under quite different conditions. In the first place it may for the most part be regarded as an autumn and winter, and not as a summer, pastime. The fish caught on open sandy beaches, chiefly cod and whiting, do not on most parts of the coast come into the shallow broken water until the turn of October, and they are gone again in most seasons by the New Year. The shore-haunting fish of summer,

346

88.—BAITING THE HOOK.

89.—A CHANGE OF GROUND.

the bass and mullet and pollack, keep to the rocks, and can only be caught from the shore in the rocky situations afore-mentioned. As already stated in these notes, I think, this wintry fishing no longer appeals to me. For me the warm summer mornings and evenings, when there is a heat haze over the western bays, and the tar is hot and soft upon the piers. Still, in other days, I, too, delighted in frosty daybreaks on Deal pier, or in crisp moon-light evenings in the Maldon reach of the Essex Blackwater; and for the sake of those who may still, youthful or otherwise, preserve such fine enthu-siasms, I gladly ransack the memories of the past for any practical hints that may therein be stored.

The rod has already been counselled as the right tackle for rock-fishing, not in any slavish adherence to rod-fishing under all sorts and conditions, which I hold to be sometimes overdone in salt water, but be-cause, as suggested in " John Bickerdyke's " amus-ing prehistoric peep, the rod was specially devised to save the line from the cutting edges of the rocks. On open shores, in fishing on the sand, the rod is a convenience to my mind only where there is a sloping shingle beach, as is, for instance, the case at Hastings at high water, close to the water's edge. The position of the angler sitting on such a slope enables him to hold the rod without discomfort, or it may even be laid down on the shingle while, in cold weather, he takes a stroll up and down to make his blood spin.

A sandy shore, on the other hand, usually comes

very gradually down to the water, and the rod is a
positive inconvenience. The hand-line, under such
conditions, may be used comfortably, and by the
simple device of a button close to the lead, and
a forked ash pole, such a line may be swung
out thirty or forty yards with ease. On the East
Coast, indeed, where this style of beach-fishing is
much practised during the autumn months, experts
will cast even farther. Fifteen or twenty hooks
may be used on such a throw-out line, and the best
bait is lugworm. Mussel would be even better,
perhaps, as far as the tastes of the cod and whiting
are concerned, but the throwing loosens the mussel
to such an extent, even if it does not jerk it right
off the hook, that the fish are able to suck the
hooks clean without the fisherman suspecting a
bite. The East Coast plan of using more than one
line cannot be recommended to any one not fishing
for the market, and indeed those whose enthusiasm
is mainly commercial would often catch more fish
and lose fewer baits if they would confine their
attention to one line only, and with fewer hooks,
half-a-dozen being quite sufficient for the amateur's
purpose. Such a line held in the hand should
enable the angler—let me call him "fisherman,"
since he has not a rod, and thus steer clear of the
hypercritical—to feel each bite, and to strike at
once and hook his fish, and the fish killed will work
out a better average per hook than if fifty hooks
were launched in this way and left for the fish
to rob.

The leger line is particularly useful on sandy ground and when fishing from a sandy beach. Its chief feature is a pierced lead, generally flat, through which, when the angler is expecting a bite, the line is free to move in one direction only, away from where he stands, its movement in the opposite direction being arrested by a split shot too large to pass the lead. The same principle, of the line running freely one way only, is involved in the somewhat lazy arrangement suggested in the next paragraph. There are various forms of leger lead, but they agree in their plan of action, or rather of inaction, for they all lie on the ground so as not to interfere in the sensitiveness of the tackle, and the readiness with which the fisherman can feel the slightest bite. A leger lead may be used with either rod or hand-line, but on the beach I prefer the latter. The hook is baited with either lugworm or mussel —the latter tied on with yellow worsted to keep it on the hook when throwing out the line—for flat-fish, or with herring or sprat for cod and whiting, and the lead is cast out as far as may be necessary. Then, if using a rod, the angler reels in line until there is no slack between the rod and lead, and the slightest bite will then be registered by the twitching of the rod top. If using the leger with a hand-line, he simply hauls in line until the same condition of tautness is arrived at, and then holds the line between the thumb and forefinger of the right hand, striking as soon as he feels a bite. Two hooks may be used in conjunction with the leger lead, one above and the other beneath it, but more than two are not advisable.

There is an excellent, though somewhat primitive, plan for obviating the exertion of throwing out whenever the fish are removed and the hooks re-baited, which may here be briefly described. A stout stake three feet long, with a ring in the top, is driven well into the sand at low water-mark up to two-thirds of its length, so that only one foot remains above the ground. The line bearing the hooks is passed through the ring, but in place of the lead there is a cross toggle of wood or a piece of wire fixed crosswise on the line, close to the last hook, and too long to pass through the ring. The line must be twice as long as the ordinary throw-out line, and, when the home end has been passed through the ring and pulled through till the further progress of the line is arrested by the wire or wooden toggle, the home end of the line is made fast to the toggle. The position is then this : the line forms an endless band, free to move in either direction through the ring until stopped by the toggle, which cannot pass. Close to the latter are ten or twelve hooks, and these, attached to the main line by six inch lengths of single gut, and of the size previously recommended for mackerel, are baited with lugworm, herring, soft crab, squid, or whatever may be handy in the list of sea-baits. It will easily be seen that the fisherman can sit com-fortably above high-water mark and continually pull the hooks towards him ; then, when they are

re-baited or the fish removed, he can, by pulling
the other side of the line, carry them out again into
the deeper water. The home end of the line may
be hitched over another stake, also driven firmly
in the ground, or through a ring let into a heavy
stone, or piece of yacht's ballast. This method
of fishing was imparted to me fifteen or sixteen
years ago by the late Mr. Wilcocks, and capital fun
I have had with it in the Hastings district, as have
others since then to whom I in turn told the details
of management. I do not know that it will bear
very strict investigation when considered as sport,
but I have long arrived at the conclusion that that
widely used term needs an occasionally more generous
interpretation than that commonly assigned to it.
So long as no unsportsmanlike method, such as
dynamite or foul-hooking, is resorted to, a man of
modest ambitions may find sport, otherwise recreation, in a style of fishing that the more fastidious
would unhesitatingly vote child's-play. Personally, I
find no amusement whatever in whiffing for mackerel,
but I would hardly condemn it as unsporting on
that account. Yet that is precisely what so many
people often do when discussing any but the forms
of fishing that they individually prefer.

Thus, the setting, or " shooting," as it is generally
called, of a long line—variously known as " trot,"
" spiller," or " bulter "—might conceivably afford
sport to some, and it is to the sandy coast that its
field of operations is perforce confined. Long lines
of nearly a mile in length and carrying many hundreds

of hooks are used by the professional fisherman, but such cumbrous tackles are quite inconvenient for any one fishing for pleasure, and a line with fifty hooks should be ample. Such a line may be home made, or such makers as Hearder, of Plymouth, would supply one with all the latest conveniences, such as patent toggles, by which, in the event for instance of a conger tangling the line, a particular hook may be removed and another substituted in a minute. The long line is usually set for market purposes in moderately deep water five or ten miles from land, but the amateur, using finer tackle and smaller hooks, may have plenty of fun with one laid between two small anchors or heavy stones along a sandy shore, and obliquely across the tide. The line must be stretched tightly between the anchors or stones, and not only must it be attached very firmly to these, but they in turn must be made fast to the ground, else loss will ensue. Nay, since human nature fell from its high estate before sea-fishing was the fashion, even these precautions are not enough. The owner must, in person or by proxy, watch through the tide to see that no one else lifts his property by mistake. Unsophisticated people believe in the practice of stamping their name or initials on the stones or anchors, but it is to be feared that this is little hindrance. The line is laid between its anchors or stones at low tide and as close to low-water mark as possible, but rather above it in case, from a change of the wind or any other cause, the following ebb tide should not uncover the sand to quite so far out. The hooks are

90.—INTO A GOOD FISH

91.—CASTING FROM THE REEL.

baited with mackerel, herring, squid, crab, shrimp, or lugworm, and it is a good plan with a small line of only fifty hooks to do this baiting on the spot, particularly as the line should be laid obliquely and not parallel with the shore, and the baiting can therefore be started at the seaward end, which will be first covered by the incoming waters. When all the hooks are baited, and the stones or anchors inspected to see that they are firm in the ground, the owner retires to dry land and watches the sea slowly cover up his property. If there are few rowing-boats in the locality he may safely go home, if desired, and return towards the next low water to recover the fish and re-bait the hooks ; but if there are many boats with prowling boatmen in possession, it is found to be an economy to remain on the beach the whole time, for some of these beachcombers are wonderfully skilful with a grapnel hook and line, dragging the bottom and lifting whatever they may find. Or it may even happen that they take out parties of guileless amateurs to catch " whiting " within a hundred yards of the beach, and these may get their leads or hooks foul of the long line. If they manage to wrench it from the ground and return to the pier or beach with the spoil, it is useful to meet them when they disembark and protest, as courteously as may be deemed necessary, against such behaviour. There is sometimes a chance of re-baiting the long line twice in daylight, when, for instance, in the long summer days, low tide occurs between four and seven, morning and evening, but it may not always be advisable to leave

the line out all night, for bigger fish are on the
prowl then and a large conger might take a fancy,
not perhaps to the small baits, but quite possibly to
one of the fish already hooked, and walk off with
the whole. Such a catastrophe, though not absolutely out of the question in daylight, is at least
highly improbable. At the same time, if the fisherman likes to put a few larger hooks and baits on his
long line in the evening he may, of course, have the
delight of finding an immense pollack or conger
flopping on the wet sand next morning, and the
excitement when, as the ebbing water gets shallower
and shallower, a dark form is seen struggling and
splashing on the line may be imagined and should be
tried, for it is a splendid antidote for the boredom
sometimes inseparable from the seaside holiday.

Another form of set line, which has the advantage
of being equally useful, either on a coast entirely of
sand or where there are only restricted areas of sand
between rocks, is that in which each baited hook is set
separately. In this case about two yards of fine but
strong line are made fast to the gut of the hook and
the other end is tied to the middle of an ordinary
stick of firewood six or seven inches long. The
stick is then buried in the wet sand near low-water
mark and the hook baited. It is surprising what a
hold wet sand has on a stick buried in this way a
foot or so below the surface. However big the fish
that gets on the hook, it is not the stick which will
come away, though the line, or gut, may of course
be broken. These single hooks can, of course, be
set in quite small patches of sand with rocks all

around, on parts of the coast where the laying of an ordinary long line would not be practicable. I do not for a moment pretend that either form of set hook comes under the head of Sport as commonly understood, but there is amusement to be derived from going the round of the hooks, like an Indian going the round of his traps, and it is a simple and inexpensive way of providing the larder with fresh fish, for good-sized cod and large flat-fish are often taken in this way, the former on the largest, the latter on the smallest, hooks, for flat-fish have a narrow mouth.

The only form of netting that can specifically be referred to a sandy beach is the shove-net for shrimps, and there is no need to devote any space to practical instruction in the use of this familiar square net at the end of a long pole, which men and women alike are seen pushing before them just behind the waves all the summer at most of our south-coast resorts. A very little practice will enable the amateur to push this implement at just the right angle and with just the right strength, so as neither to let the shrimps escape underneath it nor to bury it so far in the soft sand as to arrest further progress or break the frame. One injunction may be given, though it will hardly be necessary to the true sportsman, and that is that the hundreds of undersized little flat-fish, midgets little larger than a half-crown, be at once returned to the water. The short detention in the net, coupled with the slow advance through the water, and frequent hauls cannot injure them to any extent as would perhaps the shrimp trawl, and they will, at the start, certainly recover and grow to a more useful size, even if they do not live to breed, if given a chance.

This beach-fishing from sandy shores is chiefly confined in practice to the East Coast, particularly to the neighbourhood of Aldeburgh, Lowestoft, and Great Yarmouth. There is, however, no reason why it should not be tried elsewhere if the conditions are favourable. I shall have occasion, a little later, to draw attention to the capture of bass in this way at a seaside resort where such shore-fishing was formerly little known. There are many parts of the south coast, particularly in Hampshire and Devon, with sandy beaches like those of the East Coast, and, no doubt, at Bournemouth, at Weymouth, at Dawlish, at Teignmouth, this shore-fishing might answer in the autumn months. When we get to Cornwall, the frowning cliffs come for the most part to the water's edge, and sandy beaches are few and far between.

92.—*REELING IN THE SLACK.*

93.—FISHING FROM DEAL PIER.

CHAPTER XXXIV

SEA-FISHING FROM FIXED POSITIONS:
FISHING FROM PIERS AND HARBOURS

By F. G. Aflalo

FISHING from piers and harbours is an almost distinct branch of the sport, so many little modifications are necessary under the altered conditions. Much depends, in the first place, on whether the pier is a solid structure, like, say, the farther end of the Admiralty Pier used to be at Dover when they allowed one to fish there—an indulgence withdrawn, I believe, since the inception of the Government works some four or five years ago—or, as is more often the case, a skeleton framework of piles and girders, through which the water moves to and fro and often with a strong set, or current, one way

or the other, which may prove very dangerous to
light tackle. The solid pier is in every way preferable for fishing purposes with the exception of one
drawback, and that is that large fish are sometimes
knocked off the hook when being hauled up, as
they are apt to come roughly in contact with the
stonework, a collision which is in the highest degree
improbable in the open-work piers. With this
exception, then, everything is in favour of the solid
masonry. With the more common open-work piers,
which also involve standing on draughty gratings
which admit in opposite directions the cold air and
such valuables as may drop through, the angler is
exposed to a variety of more or less serious inconveniences. There is the risk, just alluded to, of
losing money, knives, pencil-cases, and so forth,
through the gratings. The secretive sand under
the piers at some of our popular watering-places
would, I should think, start a bank and an iron-
monger with coin and fishing gear. There is
another fruitful source of loss, for the shell-encrusted
girders and posts continually take a fancy to the
angler's lead and hooks, and refuse to part with
them. Overcrowding, particularly during the
months of August and September, is another undoubted drawback of pier-fishing; and when, in
addition, there are small boys in evidence swinging
immense leads, about half their own weight, round
their tiny heads, and delivering them with wonderful
accuracy on the ear of their neighbour to left or
right, that which was merely a nuisance may become

nothing short of a danger. I have before now seen
a large hook fairly embedded in the neck of a
peaceful loiterer in this way. There is no redress.
The small boy looks overwhelmed with contrition
—in reality he is mentally calculating how long it
will take to unhook the fellow who got in his way
and go on with his fishing—and the onlookers show
a tendency to treat the situation lightly. The one
remedy for this is either to restrict all pier-fishing
to the use of rods (though on some piers I have
known the authorities short-sighted enough to insist
on hand-lines), or else to prohibit throw-out lines
and allow only those which are quietly let down
alongside.

Not only is the rod safer in pier-fishing; it is
also far more convenient, and enables more anglers
to get to work side by side without one interfering
with the other. A man who knows the use of his
rod ought moreover to be able to save many a large
bass or pollack that, on the hand-line, would inevitably get foul of the posts and thus regain its liberty.
Of course it takes some knowledge and practice to
use a rod properly, and in the hands of the novice
the hand-line would in all probability catch more
fish. For float-fishing, by far the most killing
method of fishing from piers or harbours, except
in rough weather, a rod is practically indispensable.
I have seen a large float used with a light hand-line,
but it is at best a hybrid combination with all the
odds in favour of the fish.

On some of the East Coast piers, where much

autumn fishing is done at night, anglers complain that the pier authorities do not sufficiently provide for their comfort and safety, while the men on the herring boats declare that the amateur's lanterns on the piers mislead them when steering for harbour late at night.

It is of the greatest importance in pier-fishing that there shall be a sense of good fellowship, as otherwise it is impossible to fish in harmony. When, for instance, a number of anglers are using rods and float tackle side by side, it is necessary as soon as one hooks a really heavy fish that the others should at once reel in and stop fishing until the fish is either won or lost. Self-interest indeed dictates this policy as well as courtesy, for if the other floats be not at once hauled clear of the water, the frenzied efforts of the fish to escape will speedily entangle all the lines, and there will be no more fishing for perhaps a quarter of an hour, while the language that then will float upon the summer breeze will make the mermaids stop their shell-like ears with seaweed. The floats, too, should be dropped quietly in, at any rate when the tide is carrying them clear of the pier. There is no need to make magnificent casts from the Nottingham reel unless one has the pier to oneself, and even then the effort entailed in such feats is usually out of all proportion to the result. I have already alluded to the fact, which is within the experience of almost every amateur sea-fisherman of any experience at all, of the fish generally feeding close against the rock or against the piles of a pier; and in nine cases out of ten a float-line pitched some distance from where the angler stands will take the bait out of ken of the fish.

Float tackle or the paternoster is the best tackle for pier-fishing, and the paternoster may be used either up and down or as a throw-out line. Two other tackles, the leger and chopstick, may also be used if so desired, but the latter at any rate must be used with a rod and not with a hand-line. To throw a chopstick out and let it lie on the ground is to ignore its obvious intent and purpose, and fish will not only be very hard to hook, but even extremely chary of biting. The proper position of the chopstick is hanging on a vertical line a short distance above the ground. Now, to use a chopstick in this fashion from a pier on an ordinary hand-line would be to court the immediate risk of entanglement with the ironwork and consequent loss of gear. Only with the help of a rod is it possible to dangle the chopstick in its right position and at the same time keep it clear of the posts. And, as the chopstick is at best a heavy and cumbersome gear to use with a light rod, it had better be left for boat work with a hand-line, when large whiting-pout or silver whiting are biting furiously in deep water.

When there are large mackerel round a pier, as sometimes occurs in hot summers at Bournemouth and elsewhere on the south coast, the drift-line is a killing method of fishing, but it is essential to fish on the falling tide. August mornings when the

tide is high about four are the most promising, and
the angler fishes from, say, half-past four till seven.
A very small and lively sand-eel is the best bait, but
a strip of mackerel, little more than skin, cut as
described on an earlier page, is also deadly, and I
have even had good sport using a couple of small
mussels. For mackerel fishing from piers, whether
with the drift-line or float tackle, which is also
useful, a trout-rod is an absolute necessity. A fish
which twists and turns and dashes and sheers, like
the mackerel, is extremely dangerous among the
ironwork of a pier, and it would be quite impossible
to keep it clear of collision on a hand-line, while on
a stiff sea-rod the light gut, at least three yards of
which is necessary in this fine fishing, would in all
probability break under the sudden rushes of this
sporting fish. As, owing to the peculiar structure
of the mouth, mackerel, though to all appearance
well hooked, are very liable to fall off the hook
when hauled clear of the water, a long-handled
landing-net will save many a fish that would otherwise get away. Such a net was made for me a year
or two ago by Bernard, of Jermyn Street, and the
handle is in three pieces, making up a total length
of twelve feet or more. This might seem a cumbersome implement to use in the landing of so
small a fish as a mackerel, but it is not of course
handled like a smaller landing-net in a boat.
I make it fast to the post beside which I am
fishing, and a very little practice enables a friend
to manœuvre it, still held almost perpendicular, so

as to lessen the strain of leverage that so long a handle would otherwise throw on the hands, under the struggling fish. The net is then raised, always perpendicular, hand over hand, until the fish is recovered.

Something has been said above of the risk of loss of tackle involved in fishing from the majority of piers. This risk is usually entailed in collision with the posts or cross-girders of the pier itself. It may also happen, however, that there are small rocks or sunken piles or drain pipes in the immediate vicinity of the pier, and it is a good plan when fishing for the first time from a strange pier to make a rough-and-ready survey of the surrounding bed of the sea. This may be done quite simply and effectually, albeit without much pretence to scientific method, by tying a large stone (weighing, say, a pound) lightly to a ball of cheap string and throwing it out, as if it were a lead line, in different directions, then allowing it to sink to the bottom, and drawing it slowly back so that it travels quietly over every yard of the ground to the very edge of the pier. In this way much may be learnt of obstacles, natural or other-wise, and only the stone will be lost in place of more costly leads and hooks that must otherwise have been sacrificed at the same shrine. The fisherman will learn to avoid certain sunken traps and pitfalls, of which he will carefully take the bearings by noting the post opposite which they lie, and he will at the same time mark out for himself safe places where his lead and hooks may lie at rest. Needless to say,

these hydrographical surveys must be conducted at
an hour when there is no one else fishing.

It would hardly be possible to offer any individual
notes on the fishing to be had off most of our piers.
In the first place, the fishing from piers varies even
more than that to be obtained in boats, for an increase or decrease in steamer traffic, together with
other artificial conditions, may influence it to a
degree not felt on the outer grounds. Again, the
authorities occasionally act in a somewhat arbitrary
manner in respect of the angler and seem to experiment with his patience, at one time suddenly prohibiting rods, at another either putting a stop to
all manner of fishing for a period, or else imposing
without warning a payment for the privilege. There
is nothing to urge against this charge for fishing ;
indeed, a small fee would sometimes have the bene-
ficial result of keeping lads away who care little for
serious fishing, and only frequent pier-heads for the
pleasure of getting in every one's way. On some
piers, at Deal for instance, and at Eastbourne, at
Tenby and at the Mumbles, a small charge (threepence per rod for the day, if I remember rightly)
has long been made. On others the charges appear
to be variable in amount and arbitrary as to season,
and on one small Devon pier that shall be nameless
the zealous piermaster, acting no doubt for the good
of his employers, had a notice board in reserve on
which was printed in large type, " Good fishing at
the end of the pier ; twopence each," and this he
promptly hung over the turnstyles as soon as a

54 — *BRIGHTON PIER.*

smelt was caught at the farther end of the modest structure over which he so assiduously presided.

Most of our south-coast piers may be taken, roughly, as affording pout, sand-smelt, small flat-fish, mackerel, and at night conger, in July, August, or September, and in the winter months small whiting, with the chance of now and again a large cod. A few of them also give bass, but pier-fishing for bass is perhaps the most uncertain method of seeking an always elusive fish. The piers, or what is left of them, at Littlehampton give grey mullet, and some of the docks at Plymouth and Southampton offer the same chances with that sporting fish, though not as a rule with large specimens. Mullet of heavy weight used formerly to be caught from the Admiralty Pier at Dover, but since the War Office has taken over that port for its own machinations, the fishing has gone to a resort from which the War Office makes it its business to keep the country generally. Teignmouth pier occasionally gives a few small pollack in October, and small conger may be caught at night during the warmer months with squid bait. The promenade pier at Plymouth is much resorted to in July and August nights by bass-fishers, and some really good bass and pollack are taken up to midnight, ragworms being a favourite bait. The steamer traffic is so immense at this pier that it is surprising the fish are not frightened away altogether; but no doubt familiarity breeds contempt, else the beautiful anchorages of Plymouth Sound could never be so full of fish as they are.

There is a method of fishing from harbours or
quays on tidal rivers that is distinct from anything
that has previously been described in these sea-
fishing notes.   It will be more or less welcomed
by the novice according to his attitude in respect
of bodily exercise, for it is, the aforenamed rock-
fishing excepted, about the only form of sea-fishing
with which I am acquainted that involves walking
about.   In some estuaries, like that of the Arun at
Littlehampton or the Teign at Teignmouth, the
bass come in with the flood tide and rout among the
wooden piles for small shrimps or such other food
as they can there procure.   I never knew this method
of fishing to be followed at Teignmouth, for there
the drifting in boats out in mid-stream with the
living sand-eel bait, as already described, is the only
style of bass fishing that seems to answer, though a
few fish are also picked up with green crab bait
(locally called " peeler-crab ") from boats anchored
in the tideway.   At Littlehampton, however, where
the crab and ragworm are the only baits used, they
used to catch bass five years ago—I have not visited
the place since—by using a rod and float tackle from
the quays on the left bank, close to the railway line,
and walking up with the rising tide.   It was always
enjoined as a most important condition of a good
catch that great care should be taken to leave the
line slack enough for the float to ride quite naturally on the water and not be disturbed by any sudden
pull, but I fancy, from what I remember of the
sport, that success was more often deserved than

commanded.   Whenever a stray bass was taken, there was a rush to see the trophy that indicated the rarity of such a capture.

All the same, one never knows where the bass may, or may not, be feeding, or what bait may tempt them.   I was much struck by an article in the *Field* some time last September, in which, commenting on the fierce arguments that rage around the feeding of salmon in fresh water, the writer gave it as his opinion that sportsmen considered the problem from the too restricted standpoint of the results obtained with the fly, the minnow, and one or two other more or less orthodox baits.   There is no doubt that we are apt to generalise from meagre facts.   We try bass, for instance, which are known, or thought to be in the immediate neighbourhood, with one or other of the stock baits, the living sand-eel, the soft crab, pilchard, or perhaps ray's liver, and, these failing, we go home and declare that there are no bass.   We used to walk solemnly after our floats along those Littlehampton quays, and the soft crab dangled unappreciated on the hook. Yet quite recently, I see in the *Fishing Gazette*, a Littlehampton fisherman took eight bass in the course of two hours' fishing, and a year earlier he took just three times as many in the same time, his largest measuring not far short of 20 inches.   And how did Mr. Clarence Scott catch his bass?   Why, by throwing out his tackle from the beach, twenty or thirty yards into the sea, using a two-yard gut cast and a leger lead.   And the bait?   Simply lugworm.

Where Mr. Scott first conceived the notion of baiting with lugworm for bass I do not know, but it is
about the last bait that one would think of using
where, for instance, living sand-eel was to be had.
Yet if we too had baited with lugworm and cast
out from the beach during that weary and fish-
less September of 1897, instead of fooling up and
down the quays with the wrong tackle and the
wrong bait, even we should have taken bass and
rejoiced accordingly.

The sand-smelt, or atherine, is so excellent when
fried that many amateurs used willingly to devote
an hour or two to its capture in the warm summer
months before the British climate became what it is.
In the year of grace 1903, however, these little fish
were so scarce, appearing in twos and threes where
they had formerly been seen regularly each summer
in their hundreds, that it was not worth while fishing for them.   If, perchance, our summers resume
their old-time fairness, some fun may be had fishing
for " smelts " as they are invariably called, the true
smelt, a small cousin of the salmon, being quietly
ignored.   The correct tackle for the sand-smelt is a
very fine hand-line of silk or twine, a small pipe-lead,
weighing perhaps a quarter of an ounce, two yards of
the finest gut, such as would be used in fresh water
for roach, and a tiny hook, also of the size used for
roach.   The lead is attached between the line and
gut, and the hook comes last of all.   It is baited
with a fragment from a mussel, the yellow part that
lines the shell being best liked by the fish but least

95 —A " PERCH "

96 — OFF A HIGH PIER.

easy to keep on the hook, and the whole is then carefully let down amid the little fish, which, on favourable days are seen playing beneath the pier. If they are biting shyly, the following tactics are adopted to whet their jaded appetites. The baited hook is allowed to sink rapidly through their midst until close to the bottom, and the line is then hauled slowly in, hand over hand, in a series of jerks. These manœuvres have a wonderful effect in quickening the greed of the atherines, which dash at the bait each time. I have seen a skilful smelt-fisher, a lady by the way, hook one at each haul forty or fifty times running, a catch of a hundred being not uncommon in a morning's fishing. Years ago I used to catch these sand-smelts, in company with sand-eels, on a very light trout-rod off Bournemouth pier, but it is long since I spent a summer at that beautiful resort, and, though I pass a portion at any rate of every winter there, the "smelts" are gone with the swallows, or a little later, and I do not know how that pier, once second to none for its smelt-fishing, figures nowadays in the sport. These little atherines are very tender in the lip and may easily drop off the hook, so that care should be taken to keep them away from the posts, contact with which invariably prompts them to another struggle for liberty, and also, once they are hauled to the pier stage, they should be removed from the hook over the fishing-bag or basket, else, so quick are their movements, the chances are they will drop back through the open gratings. There

used in the old days to be a tradition to the effect
that just as one sets a thief to catch a thief, and
uses mackerel to catch mackerel, so smelt was the
best bait for smelt. I certainly remember making
some good catches with this bait, but of late years
I have noticed, down in Devonshire, that mussel
answers the purpose admirably. A fragment of
ragworm is also a very killing bait at times.

The grey mullet, about the most difficult fish
to catch in British seas, is essentially the property
of the harbour-fisher, for this fish delights in the
soft food to be found alongside quays and docks.
The finest of tackle must be used, and even the
smallest float is enough at times hopelessly to
frighten these shy fish. The ideal mullet tackle
perhaps is a very light single-gut paternoster, with
a half-ounce green pear-shaped lead and a couple of
small hooks, attached by neat and inconspicuous
knots, and without any of the brass bars or other
device that might tend to frighten the mullet. For
bait a few lively ragworms would be hard to beat,
but macaroni has been used with success at Weymouth, and I have made good catches at Leghorn
with paste flavoured with anchovy. But the mullet
of southern seas are far easier to catch than those
of colder climates. As a case in point, I recollect
a small shoal of perhaps fifty grey mullet, none
of them weighing more than a pound, collecting
round the steam-pipe of my steamer, just as the
anchors were being weighed off Mogador. I had
only just joined her in time to sail, and found a

number of passengers busily engaged in trying to catch these mullet with conger-hooks baited with pieces of fish from the cook's galley. English mullet would have been scared out into mid-Atlantic by such an indignity, but these fish merely crowded into the warm blast of the pipe, and took no notice of the baited books. Taking a small hook on gut from my pocket-book, and sending one of the children present for a piece of crumb of bread, I borrowed one of the lines, and in less than five minutes, and just as the anchors were up, and the screw churning the green water into a white mist that hid the mullet for ever from our view, I had a couple of them swimming in a ship's bucket, and somebody's children had them that evening for their dinner. The centre of grey mullet fishing in this country is, I think, Littlehampton. At all events I know of no other port at which this fish is so methodically angled for. There are, or were, men at Littlehampton who, throughout the summer, whenever the tides suited, were up and fishing at the end of the harbour works soon after dawn. Once or twice I even found myself in their company, but a few failures, together with the memories of happier luck in the Mediterranean six years earlier, soon weaned me of that passion. At the same time, the grey mullet is eminently worth the sea-angler's best efforts, and I am not sure but I may give it a week or two yet at Weymouth or some other favourite haunt. These problems only want a little effort. Five years ago I wrote, as I

thought, that the bass was a vanishing fish and
hardly to be reckoned seriously except as angels'
visits; yet, for the last three years, when circumstances happen to have brought me and the bass
together, I have been out fishing scores of times for
nothing else, and have, on the whole, met with my
share of luck.

It is all important, for both the angler's own peace
of mind and that of his friends, to recollect how
great a share luck must always have in the success
or failure of the sea-angler. I do not say that it is
everything. It is not. Many a man will hook a
fine fish and lose it from sheer inexperience of how
to bring it to the net or gaff. What I mean by
laying this stress on luck is that, other things being
equal, and given the same knowledge of the subject,
one may have luck and the other may not. The
first will fill his boat with fish, or even his end of
the boat, and the other will catch nothing. On
the other hand, however, given equal luck, the man
who knows how to fish will score against the man
who does not. That is always the consolation of
the expert. It may be that the energies decline,
and that the veteran is no longer able to face the
cold blasts and long exposure; nay, even the fighting strength of big fish may be too much for his
waning muscle. Well, he must brood, not with
aught of envy or uncharitableness, over the fire or
in the sun-bathed garden of his old age, and must
console himself with talking over the old battles in
exchange for the new ones. Sometimes he will find

a new wrinkle worthy of ungrudged admiration.
Sometimes, again, he will chuckle over the greater
catches of his youth, when fish were more, and
fishermen less, plentiful than now.   There are
compensations on both sides.   The vigour of youth
and the experience of age stand in different shoes.
"Si jeunesse savait; si vieillesse pouvait"—the
saddest rubric ever penned, yet not without its
bright side.

CHAPTER XXXV

SOME NOTES ON BAITS

By F. G. Aflalo

It seems desirable that a few notes should here be given on one or two of the more uncommon natural baits, of which the sea-angler from time to time avails himself. Every form of fishing has its own peculiar natural baits, from the bluebottle or daddy-long-legs of the surreptitious trout fisherman, to the "hellgramite" stone cat-fish, and young frog of the American expert at black bass; and the sea fisherman on our coasts has as extensive a choice as most of his craft. There are all manner of fish and parts of fish, such as the tail of the eel or the liver of the ray. Few of our sea-fish are quite unimportant as bait; but the amateur may be emphatically warned not to use any of the flat-fish (save occasionally a very small living dab for bass), or gurnard, or dory, or cod, or whiting, or conger. It is with the more oily and more silvery fish that he will have most success, and such fishes as the herring, pilchard, sprat, mackerel, and sand-eel, combine these qualities which appeal alike to the fish that hunt their food by scent and those which rely on their sight to guide them to their prey. Then, after the fishes, there are many invertebrate marine animals which make excellent baits. Among crustaceans there are the prawn, the shrimp, the hermit-crab, and the soft shore-crab. The molluscs furnish mussels, limpets, oysters, razor-fish, squid, and cuttle. The annelids are represented by the lugworm, the ragworm, and the rockworm, a nereid with pincers, also found in the shells of hermit-crabs, or crawling among the bunches of mussels that cluster beneath many of our south-coast piers. This nereid worm is a most interesting creature. With its small black nippers it is able to inflict a sharp, though not in any way painful or dangerous, pinch on the finger, and the retractile action of this organ may be tested by holding the loop of a gut line within reach, when it will promptly be drawn into the ever-active mouth. It always used to be a tradition, when I fished a good deal at Dover ten or eleven years ago, that these rockworms—so called in that locality because they are chiefly procured from the rocks at the foot of the lately menaced Shakespeare Cliff —were extremely delicate, that they would only bear the ordeal of travel with considerable risk, and that they were most difficult to keep. Sunlight and fresh water were regarded as particularly damaging. Such are the notions which easily gain acceptance, and until quite recently I implicitly subscribed to the current opinions regarding the rockworm's fragile constitution. It happened, however, that I had occasion last autumn to procure a consignment of rockworms from my old friend and angling comrade, Surgeon-General Paske, of Dover, to fish for pollack with off a Devon pier. By a succession of untoward circumstances, such as the worms arriving late on Saturday, and having in consequence to be kept until the Monday, as well as by their having been forgotten for two hours in the full sun of a September afternoon and left out a whole night in a pouring rain, these unhappy worms were in turn subjected to every indignity calculated to make them leave this life. As a matter of fact, however, they were perfectly fit and lively on the Monday evening, and a few of them even survived for use on the Tuesday. Thus they showed themselves indifferent to a journey of some hundreds of miles in a perforated box sent by parcel post, as well as to all the other inconveniences here detailed. They may be hooked just through the head, and pollack of any size will dash at them and swallow them whole. The ragworm is a less fascinating annelid, commonly dug from the ooze of estuaries and harbours. It is chiefly used as a bait for smaller pollack, as also for smelts or shoals of young bass, while for the grey mullet

97.—OCTOPUS.

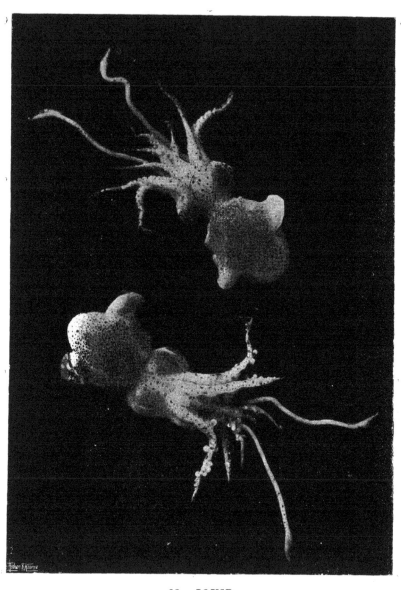

98.—SQUID.

it is usually regarded as second to none. The lugworm, coarsest and most repellent of all, is dug
deep in the sand near low-water mark, and it is
accepted by all manner of sea-fish, from large bass
down to small flat-fish. All of these worms are
best kept in shallow wooden boxes, such as would
hold fifty cigars (though the smell of the tobacco
must be thoroughly got rid of), under a covering
of green seaweed. This weed should be kept damp
with sea-water, but this must be drained off after
each wetting, as an accumulation of water in the
box seems to injure the worms. It is also desirable
that dead or injured individuals should be from
time to time removed. The ragworms are undoubtedly cannibals, and I think the same holds
good of the rockworms, but I never caught lugworms in the act of destroying one another. Indeed, their manner of feeding is different, and they
are less carnivorous than the others.

The chief baits among the molluscs are the
mussel and the squid. The mussel is familiar to
every one who has visited the seaside, though if
there are neither rocks nor a pier of some kind in
the locality it may be necessary to wait until a gale
throws up bunches of these useful shellfish on the
beach. Some of our piers, like that at Bournemouth, furnish incredible supplies of mussels, and
for the last twenty years the stock seems to have
been inexhaustible, though protected by no local
bye-law, as at Southend and at some other resorts.
There is a right way of opening a mussel, and there

are half-a-dozen wrong ways, almost any one of which is liable to result in a badly cut finger. The right way may be learnt from a fisherman in a few moments, and it would be waste of space to attempt any detailed instructions in this place.

The squid, which is not unlike an octopus, except that it has fewer arms, or tentacles, must be procured from the trawlers, or else caught by the amateur for his own use. This repulsive animal is endowed with an irrepressible curiosity, often fatal to itself, as a result of which it may be caught at sunset on a piece of white china armed with several hooks which have had the barbs filed off. The barbs would never penetrate the tough flesh of this mollusc, and even without them the points must be kept very sharp. This bait is worked in a series of jerks among the rock pools from a boat, and the squid, which seizes it with a backward dart, must be got as soon as possible to the landing-net, and carefully held beneath the surface until it has discharged the abominable cargo of ink-like fluid, with which it blinds its pursuers or victims, as circumstances may demand. It is then killed by a blow or two from a stick, cut open, washed, and cleaned. It is the first of all baits for conger fishing, and there are times when it takes some beating for dabs, whiting, or even bass.

The soft shore-crab, which has to be sought in summer under stones, where it hides away from its powerful foes in abject fear until its new armour is grown, is a first-rate bait in some places for bass and flounders, and may also be used for cod and whiting. It is usually put on the hook minus its limbs, and it is more merciful to tread on it first, thus at once killing it and making it more palatable as bait.

Edible crabs are, while in this transitional state, which goes by a variety of names, protected by the different Sea Fisheries Districts, but the angler may take the small soft green crabs of our foreshores with a clear conscience, as these are commercially valueless.

The hermit-crab is not used in many localities, but I have at times found it excellent on leger-tackle for flat-fish. In its shell, by the way, there often dwells the nereid worm above alluded to, and the shells of any hermit-crabs (stolen or borrowed, by the way, from whelks) should always be very carefully cracked and the spiral, convoluted end examined in case one of these invaluable worms should be tucked away in it. And it is surprising in how small a space these worms are able to secrete themselves.

The prawn and shrimp are usually put on the hook alive, the point being passed just through the first joint above the tail, so as to interfere as little as possible with the creature's natural movements in the water. They are taken chiefly by pollack, and at Selsey and one or two other places pollack fishers use nothing else.

The manner of taking, keeping, and using the sand-eel has already been given in sufficient detail, and it is here only necessary to add that it is, when

living, the very finest all-round bait in the sea.   If
I had to name two others for a place, I would choose
the mussel and lugworm, but I would rather any
day go afloat for really large fish with half-a-score
of lively sand-eels than with a bucket of mussels
or a hundred worms.

Herring, pilchard, and mackerel are used almost
similarly, the one peculiar bait being the small
piece from the side of the mackerel's tail, used in
mackerel fishing, and already described under its
local names of "float," "last," or "snade."   Otherwise, the two sides are removed as neatly as possible
from the backbone, the head and tail being also
cut clean off.   Then pieces, varying from half an
inch to an inch wide, according to the size of the
hooks that have to be baited, are cut diagonally
from each side.   The object of this diagonal cutting
is to give a longer strip than would be possible if
the side of the fish were cut straight across, and
also, in the case of the mackerel, to have the skin
on the bait as variegated and consequently as con-
spicuous as possible in the water.

The majority of sea-fish like the bait to be quite
free of taint.   The bass is about the only fish with
which I am acquainted that does not show itself
fastidious over a bait that is a little repulsive to
the human nose—indeed it may even be said to
prefer it in that condition.   It is generally held
that the red mullet, most delicious of sea-fish, like-
wise takes its meals "high," but as one does not
as a rule angle specially for this fish, the knowledge

is not of much practical use.   For conger, however, the squid must be absolutely sweet; for pollack or bream the pilchard must be free of decay; for flat-fish and whiting the worms should be living and the mussels newly opened.

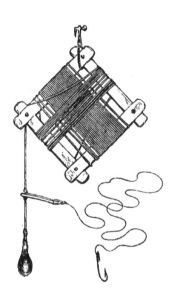

CHAPTER XXXVI

FISHERY LAWS

By J. W. Willis Bund

FOR some mysterious reason the law on all sporting matters is complicated and difficult of clear
statement, but the worst of all is the law of fishing.
The number of the Acts of Parliament, the abominable method of legislation by reference which has
been so largely used, the various local by-laws
which each small fishery board has framed for its
district, make up a collection of laws " that pass

man's understanding." The difficulty is not lessened by the fact that some laws only apply to some fish, some to others, and that to really understand the fishery laws a certain amount of biological knowledge is required. Thus the Queen's Bench held that every one was bound to know it was illegal to take the young of salmon, but no one was bound to know what fish were the young of salmon.

The best way to deal with the subject will be to state the law which is general, and prevails over all parts of England and Wales, then the law which applies only to particular places.

The general law is of two kinds, that which comes from the common law and that which comes from statute. The common law part is that which gives rise to questions as to the ownership of a right to fish, the statute law defines how the right is to be used.

(a) COMMON LAW RIGHTS.

The law regards a river, lake, arm of the sea, or any other water in the same light as it regards land, and applies the same rules of ownership to it. It is only so much land covered by water, the fact that it is so covered makes no difference to the legal incidents which attach to it. There has been some doubt expressed, but it is now settled law that all water, that is, all land covered with water, where the tide does not *regularly* ebb and flow, is private property, and the public as such have no legal

right over it.   Who is the owner is a question that
depends on circumstances, but there is an owner,
and it is his private property to the exclusion of
every one else.   The old idea that the fishing in
navigable rivers and lakes, and even large ponds,
was public has no longer any legal basis.   All non-
tidal water is private property.   It is true the
public often fish without any leave and without any
interruption, but this is only by the owner's consent ;
he could, if he liked, stop any of them at any time.
They have no right there.   In tidal waters it is
different.   The fact of the water being tidal does
not of itself alter the right of ownership ; unless the
water is not only tidal but also navigable, then
private ownership ceases, and any of the king's
subjects have the right to fish in any legal way.
This is the general rule, but there are exceptions.
Private fisheries exist in navigable tidal waters, but
they only do so under "grant charter or immemorial usuage."   The reason for this distinction as
to fishing rights arises from the ownership of soil
and the rights connected with ownership.   In all
waters not tidal and navigable the soil covered with
water belongs to an individual or individuals.   It is
a rule of law that the public as such can claim no
right to take anything from private property, so
they cannot take fish which while they are on the
owner's land belong to him.   But in tidal and navigable rivers the rule is, that the Crown as represent-
ing the public is the owner of the soil, and so the
public when fishing there are fishing on their own

99.—"TEED UP" ON THE ROCK'S FACE.

100.—*A SPIT OF LAND JUTTING OUT INTO THE RIVER.*

land. This rule depends on a case reported by Lord Coke, which is full of the technical learning of his day. In legal terms it is thus stated, the public cannot acquire by prescription a profit *à prendre in alieno solo.*

The doctrine is far-reaching; it gets rid of the notion that the public can fish in canals, from towing-paths, from boats, from a bridge, from a road. The rule is positive; the public cannot legally fish as of right in any non-tidal water, and can fish only in such tidal waters as are navigable, and have not been granted to individuals by the Crown by a grant dated before Magna Carta.

Such is the general rule as to fishing rights. A much more difficult question now arises, Who are the owners of private fishing rights? The broad rule is, the owner of the land adjoining the water. If it is a brook or a river the rule is that the brook or river belongs to the owner of the adjoining land as far as his land extends. If he owns both banks then the whole of the brook or river belongs to him as far as his ownership of both banks goes. If he only owns one bank then his ownership only extends to the centre of the stream or river. This rule settles the law as to all streams and rivers, unless both tidal and navigable, and quite independent of the width; it is a rule of law, and whoever disputes it has to prove the contrary. This may be done, but it rests with the claimant to do it. This rule does not apply to pools and lakes, there it is left to each party to prove what belongs to him and where his boundary goes, just as it would be on any other piece of land. In tidal navigable rivers the whole of the bed of the river from bank to bank belongs to the Crown unless the contrary can be proved.

Fishing rights are divided into three kinds. More has been written, and more confusion has arisen as to the precise definition of these three rights, than can be imagined. The first is called a *several fishery*; it is the most common form of right, the one possessed by every land-owner to keep his fishery several, separate, and apart from every one else. It is a right that implies either that the person who owns it also owns the soil, or that his right has been derived in some way from the owner of the soil. Until the contrary is proved, every owner of a fishery is presumed by law to own a separate or several fishery.

With the second the confusion begins; it is called a *free fishery*. Naturally persons have considered this means a fishery where any one could fish, but the meaning is very different. What the precise meaning is no two lawyers are agreed upon. All are agreed that it is a private fishery; but one class say, and, most likely, correctly, that it means a right to fish in another man's water by virtue of a royal grant, precisely as a " free warren " means a right to take game on another man's land by virtue of a royal grant. If this meaning is adopted things are fairly clear, but if the other meaning, that it is a peculiar kind of several fishery differing from it in certain of its incidents, the confusion is tremendous. Practically, it may be said that a free fishery is an exclusive right of fishing which has in its origin nothing to do with the ownership of the soil, and which may even exclude the owner of the soil from fishing on his own land.

The third right has also a very confusing name, a *common fishery*. Persons naturally, and Parliament also, have jumped to the conclusion that a common fishery means a public fishery, and speaks in the Salmon Fishery Act, 1873, of a " Public or Common Fishery " as if they were synonymous. No idea could be more mistaken. A " common fishery," or to speak more correctly, a " common of fishery," is a private fishery, but one where rights of common may be exercised by the tenants of a manor. Precisely in the same way as commoners exercise rights of pasture over the wastes of the manor, so they exercise rights of common of fishery over the water of the manor. A common of fishery is not very usual, but it does exist in some places, and here the commoners have the right of fishing in the lords' waters. For practical purposes any right of fishing may be treated as a several fishery, that is the legal presumption, and if any one alleges the contrary he must prove it. The ownership of the land implies the ownership of the fishing.

At common law every one could take his fish as he pleased, there was nothing to prevent him doing so, at all times, in all places, and by all modes he thought fit. By statute various restrictions have been placed on the rights of owners as to fishing, both as to times, places, and modes. The statute law of fishing is the history of these restrictions.

(*b*) STATUTE LAW.

The restrictions are of two kinds : general, those that apply to all fish whether in private or public waters; partial, those that only apply to particular fish, particular modes of fishing, or particular places.

The restrictions go back to the earliest times. Two sections of Magna Carta provide against the Crown granting private fisheries in public waters, and against the erection of weirs in navigable rivers. From that time to the present, Act after Act of Parliament has been passed imposing restrictions on fishing. As to salmon, the majority were repealed in 1861, but since then no less than sixteen statutes have become law placing restrictions on fishery rights. As regards fish other than salmon and trout, most of the restrictions have been imposed by modern legislation, dating from 1878.

The chief of the general restrictions, which apply to all fisheries and to all fish are :—

(*a*) *Times of Fishing.*—With the exception of mature eels, all fish that are found in inland waters have a close time, during which it is unlawful to catch or to sell them. This close time varies for different kinds of fish. Thus salmon have one, trout another, coarse fish another, young eels and

elvers another, all fixed by statute, and most of these
statutory times can be locally varied by by-laws;
but whatever the variations, it may be taken that
in all places in England and Wales there is a close
time during each year when fish cannot be taken.
A list of these close times is given below.

(*b*) *Places of Fishing.*—By statute no fishing weir
can now be erected in any navigable river in England
or Wales. Whether a person can erect a new weir
in a non-navigable river for fishing purposes is a
point that has not been expressly decided. The
balance of authority would seem to be against it.
The point was raised in a modern case, argued but
not decided. Still less has the point been settled
whether, in a non-navigable river, an existing weir
which has no fish trap can be altered into a weir
with a fish trap for fish other than salmon. The
whole tendency of modern law is against the creation
of new fixed fishing traps.

(*c*) *Modes of Fishing.*—No person can use dynamite or other explosive substances to kill fish. This
applies to the owner, equally as to any one else. No
person can use any fish roe for fishing for any kind
of fish. No person can use poison to kill or destroy
fish.

These prohibitions are universal, and apply in all
parts of England and Wales.

As to *partial* restrictions, these are also general
and local. The general apply throughout all
England and Wales (except to the Tweed district),
unless they have been locally varied as to particular

fish. The most important are those as to salmon. For this purpose salmon has a very wide meaning, and applies not merely to salmon as popularly understood, but to all *migratory* fish of the genus " salmon," whatever may be the local name ; this includes salmon, sea trout, white trout, and all trout that migrate to the sea. Whether it includes trout that migrate from one part of the river to another at certain times of the year has never been definitely settled.

The restrictions fall within two heads :—The modes of killing salmon ; the times of killing salmon.

The prohibited modes are the use of poisonous substances which may sicken or kill fish—the use of poaching methods such as lights, spears, otters, stroke hauls, or gaffs. The use of all but the last is absolutely, the improper use of the last is only, forbidden. The use of proper methods in an improper way—the chief of these are the use of fixed engines ; the use of fishing weirs or dams ; the use of nets with too small a mesh, the standard mesh being two inches from knot to knot. There are a series of provisions restricting the mode of using legal nets, such as they may not be used near a weir or dam, nor in a mill-race, nor too closely together, nor in a way to unduly increase their normal catching power. Under this head are included the provisions for the construction of fixed engines, fishing weirs, and fishing mill-dams. Certain of these restrictions can be increased by by-laws, a power which has been locally exercised in many cases.

There are also provisions forbidding taking salmon out of season, or even in season if in an unfit state to be taken, technically called "unclean," or of young salmon before they have migrated to the sea, or of disturbing spawning salmon, or beds on which they have spawned. There are also a series of restrictions as to the time when salmon may be taken. The rule, unless altered by by-laws, is that no salmon may be taken in England and Wales between the 1st September and the 1st February following, both inclusive, by net, or any means other than rod and line, and that no salmon may be taken by rod and line except between the 1st of February and the 1st of November, both days inclusive. As to sale, salmon caught after the first of September cannot be sold unless the person who offers it for sale can prove that the fish was caught at some place where the capture for sale was legal. Salmon taken with rod and line after the 1st September cannot be legally sold. In order to give salmon a chance of ascending rivers no fishing except with rod and line is legal between noon on Saturday and 6 A.M. on the next Monday. This is the minimum. By by-laws this has been extended in certain districts. And in one case as to certain fixed engines, in consideration of their not beginning to fish before the 1st May, they are allowed to fish continuously until the end of the season without regard to weekly close time.

Certain of the provisions as to salmon are extended to trout and char. These are prohibiting certain modes of taking these fish, such as lights, spears, gaffs, otters, and stroke hauls, taking, killing, or injuring unclean or unseasonable trout or char, and a close time, extending from the 2nd October to 2nd February, but which has been increased and varied in some localities, during which it is illegal to take or sell trout or char.

There are also a series of provisions by which the consignment or exportation of salmon, trout, or char during close time is made illegal.

The next class of restrictions are in regard to fresh-water fish, which are all fish living permanently or temporarily in fresh waters other than salmon.

Except close time, which is from the 15th March to the 15th June, both inclusive, during which it is illegal to take or sell any fresh-water fish other than pollan trout or char and eels, there is no general statutory restriction as to fresh-water fish as such.

The special restrictions as to fish are the local by-laws made by the Board of Conservators for each of the different fishery districts. They can be made for the following purposes :—

For Salmon — (*a*) Altering the annual and weekly close time for salmon and the annual close time for trout.

(*b*) Determining the length, size, and description of nets, the manner of using them, the minimum size of the mesh, and the marks or labels

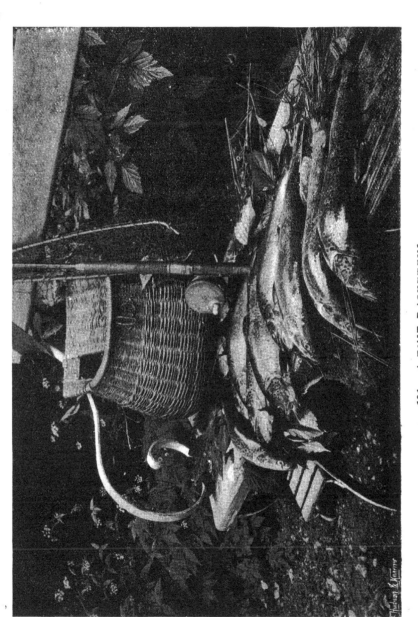

101.—A FINE BASKETFUL.

102.—CHOOSING THE FLY.

to be fixed to nets or fishing-boats. Prohibiting the use of nets at the mouths of rivers. Determining the times when a gaff may be used with a rod and line, when gratings should be placed at mill-races. Regulating fishing for fish other than salmon during the annual and weekly close time. Prohibiting netting at night.

For Fresh-water Fish.—Determining the minimum size of the mesh of nets, the length, size, and description of nets that may be used, and the manner of using them. Prohibiting the use of any mode or instrument of fishing if the use appears prejudicial to the fisheries.

These powers are exercised by bodies known as Boards of Conservators, or Fishery Boards. They consist of three classes of members :—

(1) *Ex-officio* those who have a certain length of river frontage and pay license duty, and those who are assessed for fisheries of the value of £30 a year.

(2) *Elected* persons, elected by the holders of net licenses which are used in public fisheries.

(3) *Appointed* persons, nominated by the County Councils and by the councils of county boroughs in the watershed.

These form the Board ; they are elected annually. The limit of their jurisdiction is their fishery district which consists of the whole or part of one or more watersheds as may be included in the certificate forming the district. Originally the duty of forming districts was assigned to the Home Office, then to the Board of Trade, and now to the Board of Agriculture and Fisheries.   The control of all the fisheries in their districts is vested in the Local Board.   Their duties are :—To appoint a sufficient number of water-bailiffs to look after the fisheries ; to issue licences for fishing ; to purchase by agreement any weirs, in order to remove them ; to take legal proceedings for the violation of the Fishery Acts; to erect fish passes, gratings, and other works for the preservation of the fisheries ; to make by-laws.

To furnish these Boards with funds to carry out their duties they are empowered to levy licenses for fishing for salmon, trout, and char, but not for other fish.   These licenses are sold at fixed prices, the maximum in some cases being fixed in the Act; if it is not, the Board fixes it, subject to approval of the Board of Agriculture.   Licenses must be sold to any one who asks for them, but they do not give a purchaser any right to fish.   While he cannot catch or fish for salmon, trout, or char without a license, the fact that he has a license does not give him leave to fish.   This he must get independently.   In this respect the license is like one to kill game, but it differs from it in this very important respect, a game license is a license to kill game by any lawful means, a fish license only authorises the holder to fish with the particular instrument named in it.   A licensee who had a rod license could not use a net, and *vice-versâ*.   Indeed, he can only use one instrument of the class named. Thus an angler who fishes for trout and uses two rods at the same time requires two licenses.

In a fishery district it is always best to take out a license for a rod and line for trout. The cost is usually very small, 1s. or 2s. 6d., and it saves the very troublesome question that is often arising but has as yet never been actually decided. If a person goes out fishing for what he can catch in a river containing trout and other fish, and uses a rod and line with a bait equally calculated to take trout as well as other fish, does he require a license? The case has come on several occasions before the court, but the magistrates have always found as a fact that the angler either was or was not fishing for trout, so that the real question has not been raised before the court.

Although there are still in England and Wales some places that are not in a fishery district, and so no license is required, these are very few, and the general rule is that if a person fishes for trout he must have a license; but the law goes farther, even if he has a license it must be for the method of fishing he is using. Thus a person angling with a license would not be entitled to catch trout with his landing-net independently of his rod and line. Some Boards of Conservators, to stop the use of what they think poaching modes of fishing, such as night-lines, refuse to license them. The result is that any one who uses a night-line for trout in that district makes himself liable to a penalty for fishing for trout without a duly licensed instrument. As the rule applies equally to the owner as to other persons, it follows that the owner cannot legally bale out holes in his own brook and take trout, as baling out trout or taking them by the hands is not a licensed mode of fishing in any fishery district. This rule also applies to salmon. A person who takes, as can be done in a tidal estuary, a live salmon out of a pool left by the tide incurs a penalty for taking a salmon without a license. But a person who picks up a dead salmon on the sands does not require a license. It would be impossible to state all the pitfalls for the unwary that the law as to licenses provides. As already stated, the only way to be safe is to take out a license.

These are the main statutory provisions of the Fishery Acts. There are also certain matters in other Acts that should be noticed. By the Larceny Law Consolidation Act, 1861 (24 and 25 Vict., c. 96), it is an indictable offence to take fish in any water running through or in land adjoining a dwelling-house. It is an offence punishable on summary conviction to take fish in any other water where there is a private right of fishing, otherwise than by angling in the daytime. In the case of angling in the daytime the offence is also punishable summarily, but the penalty is less. As to angling, the owner is by the same statute empowered to seize the trespasser's rod and tackle, but if this is done no legal proceedings can be taken. It should be noticed that the power is only given to the *owner* or any one authorised by him. A tenant, unless authorised by the owner, would not have the right. Care should be always taken by the tenant to have such a power expressly given him in his lease. The

seizure can only be made on the ground, water, or
fishery of the owner, so that a trespasser, if wading, if
only half the river was included in the lease, has only
to step over the middle line to prevent the power
being exercised. Care must also be taken not to
seize too much; it is only the rod, line, hook, net, or
other implement that can be seized; if anything
else is taken, such as the fish caught, the person
who seizes would be liable to an action for damages.
A person found angling in the day is, for this section,
a person found between the beginning of the last
hour before sunrise and the expiration of the first
hour after sunset.

To protect the fisheries and see that the law is
carried out Fishery Boards appoint water-bailiffs.
These officers have very large and very arbitrary
powers. They have a right to enter upon and
examine all weirs, engines, and traps for taking
fish; to stop and search boats, to seize all articles
forfeited under the Fishery Acts; to search all nets,
baskets, and bags used in carrying fish. On this a
question has arisen, and not been as yet decided, if
a water-bailiff can search pockets as a police constable can under the Poaching Prevention Acts. The
Acts give a water-bailiff all the powers of a constable,
but it is doubtful if these extend the right given by
a special statute to search for game to the right to
search for fish. The Acts also authorise a water-
bailiff to obtain from the Fishery Board power to
enter and remain on land and to get a search-
warrant to search houses. A power is also given

to arrest persons found illegally fishing at night. Before sunset a person can only be asked for his name and address, and whether he gives a true or false address he cannot be arrested; but a person angling at night, or a person found fishing by any means other than angling, may be arrested.

Proceedings under this section of the Larceny Act often fail because the offender set up what was known as a *bonâ-fide* claim of right to fish at the place in question, and if he could get the justices to believe this, their jurisdiction was ousted. Recent decisions have, however, prevented this defence being of the same use as formerly. It has been decided that a mere *bonâ-fide* belief that the defendant has a right will not do, he must prove (*a*) that the right he claims is a right that can legally exist, and (*b*) give some evidence, very slight evidence will do, of its legal existence. Thus a claim to fish in non-tidal waters as one of the public, which was the usual case, will not do, as such a right cannot exist in law. But if it was a claim to fish at the place as an individual and some evidence, either documentary or oral, could be given of the individual's right, then the justices could not go on with the case. Two other points may be noticed; the Larceny Act makes it an offence to take fish in any private fishery, whether in tidal or non-tidal waters, provided it can be shown the fishing is private. Only if it is in tidal waters the complainant must prove his right; in non-tidal waters, all he need show is his ownership of the spot, or that he is occupier of it under a deed without reference to title. It will then be for the defendant to justify his fishing. The other point is, that the term fish in the section is not limited to fish popularly so called ; it includes every fish, and probably all living inhabitants of the fishery, even if not properly speaking fish, such as crayfish.

Fish that have been caught and are placed in a pond, or boat, or tank, so that they can be taken out when desired, are the private property of the owner, and any one who takes them can be indicted for larceny. In George I.'s reign an Act, known as the " Black Act," was passed, which made it a capital felony for persons at night to cut down the bank or sluice of a fish pond. This provision has been repealed, but by the Malicious Injuries to Property Act, 1861 (24 and 25 Vict., cap. 97), it is still a misdemeanour, punishable with seven years' penal servitude, to cut or break down the bank of a fish pond in which there is a private right of fishing, with intent to take or destroy the fish, or to place lime or other noxious material in any pond or water in which there is a private right of fishing, to destroy fish.

There are provisions under the Salmon Fishery Act against polluting a salmon river or its tributary, but they are so fenced round with provisoes, one of which is that it is necessary to prove that fish were actually sickened or killed by the pollution, as to render them almost useless. The Rivers' Pollution Prevention Act also purports to deal with pollution, but except in regard to solid matters the difficulties and restrictions as to proceedings under it, especially the action of the Local Government Board in the way it protects polluters, render the Act of very little practical use. The only really effective way to prevent pollution is an action for an injunction in the High Court of Justice, but this, although efficient, is a very costly form of procedure.

In prosecutions before justices, which are the usual form that fishery litigation takes, the prosecutor, if he is the tenant, must remember that, unless he has a lease of the fishing rights by a deed, that is by a document under seal, he has no legal right to prosecute, and a prosecution by him against a trespasser must, if the objection was taken, be dismissed. Rights of the class to which fishing rights belong only pass by deed. There is also this very important point to be remembered that, by statute, shooting rights, that is, rights to the game, are given to the occupier, unless expressly reserved, but the Act does not apply to fishing rights, and as to these the question is, Do they belong to the landlord or his tenant? This turns on the question under what does the tenant hold? If he holds by a lease or agreement, under seal, then the question is whether on the wording of that agreement the fishing has been given the tenant, not whether it has been reserved to the landlord? Unless the landlord has reserved the right to enter on the land to fish, he may not be able to exercise the right, or give a lessee of the fishery the power to exercise the right, but in law the right to fish does not necessarily pass to the tenant. Unless the document under which the tenant holds is under seal, it is clear that the right remains in the landlord. A tenant of fishing rights should, therefore, always make sure of two things— (1) Whether the right of fishing is legally in the hands of the landlord or tenant; and (2) That he gets an instrument under seal from whoever has the right of granting it to him. If he does not do this he may see the best part of his fishery fished, as he was going fishing, by a poacher, and not be able to prevent him doing so. For he is only a licensee, and can do nothing but enjoy the permission given to him. It is true that these points do not often arise, but that they may do so should make a person who pays for a fishery see that he gets it.

As has already been mentioned, it is impossible to get a conviction before justices against a trespasser who sets up a *bonâ-fide* claim of right. In taking a fishing great care should be exercised to see that this mode of poaching cannot be used. To go to the cost of turning down fish, and to find that a costly action is the only way to prevent them being poached by some claimant of an utterly absurd right, is an example of the *sic vos non vobis* doctrine that is far from pleasant. Another point to be guarded against is that of the occupier of the land giving leave to fish. Farm boys naturally poach, and say they have their master's leave. In a number of cases it would be very difficult to prove that this was not so, especially if the fishing tenant was not on good terms with the farmer. In such a case, unless it can be proved clearly that the occupier had no right to give leave, it would not be easy to get a conviction.

Numberless other points as to the difficulty of effectually protecting fishing rights, if they are rented, may be given. The only safe way is to get a document under seal to which all persons who might set up adverse claims are parties. It may be troublesome and expensive to get, but it is less troublesome and less expensive than the disputes that will follow if it is not obtained.

Local Fishery Laws.

In various places there are in force additions and alterations to the general laws, in some cases under local Acts of Parliament, in others under local by-laws. Local acts used to be very numerous, but for practical purposes only three groups need now be considered,—these are the Tweed, the Thames, and Norfolk and Suffolk. Local by-laws are in force in all the fishery districts, and of these a tabular summary is given which will suffice to give an idea of what the law is in different places.

The local laws relating to fisheries may be thus summarised :—

In England and Wales.—As to salmon the annual close time has been varied in the following districts, in all others it remains as fixed by statute,

103 — BRINGING HIM IN

Sept. 1 to Feb. 1, both days inclusive, for nets, and Nov. 1 to Feb. 1 for rods :—

District.	Nets.	Rods.
Adur	...	Oct. 1 to Feb. 2.
Avon (Devon) .	Sept. 30 to May 1	Nov. 30 to May 1.
Avon and Stour .	July 31 to Feb. 1	Oct. 2 to Feb. 1.
Axe	Sept. 20 to April 30	Nov. 20 to April 30.
Ayron	...	Nov. 15 to Feb. 14.
Camel	Sept. 21 to April 4	Dec. 1 to April 30.
Cleddy	Sept. 15 to March 15	Nov. 1 to Feb. 1.
Conway . . .	Sept. 15 to April 30	Nov. 15 to April 30.
Coquet	Sept. 15 to March 25	Nov. 1 to Jan. 31.
Dart.	Sept. 1 to March 12	Oct. 16 to Feb. 28.
Dee	Sept. 1 to March 31	Nov. 2 to March 31.
Derwent . . .	Sept. 15 to March 10	Nov. 15 to March 10.
Dovey	Sept. 14 to April 30	Nov. 1 to April 30.
Dwyfach . . .	Sept. 15 to March 1	Nov. 15 to March 1.
Eden	Sept. 10 to Feb. 10	Nov. 16 to Feb. 15.
Elwy and Clwyd	Sept. 15 to May 15	Nov. 15 to May 15.
Exe	Sept. 1 to March 1	Oct. 20 to March 1.
Fowey	Nov. 1 to April 4	Dec. 1 to April 30.
Kent.	Sept. 15 to March 31	Nov. 15 to March 31.
Lune	Sept. 1 to March 1	Nov. 2 to March 1.
Ogmore . . .	Sept. 15 to April 30	Nov. 15 to April 30.
Ouse (Sussex) .	Sept. 1 to April 1	Nov. 1 to April 1.
Rhymney . . .	Sept. 1 to April 1	Nov. 2 to April 1.
Ribble	Sept. 1 to March 1	Nov. 2 to March 1.
Seiont	Sept. 15 to March 1	Nov. 15 to March 1.
Severn	Aug. 15 to Feb. 1	...
Stour (Canterbury)	Sept. 1 to May 1	Nov. 2 to May 1.
Taff and Ely . .	Aug. 31 to April 30	Nov. 15 to April 30.
Taw and Torridge	Sept. 21 to April 30	Nov. 16 to March 31.
Teign	Sept. 1 to March 2	Nov. 1 to March 2.
Towy	Sept. 1 to April 1	Oct. 15 to April 1.
Usk	Sept. 1 to March 1	Nov. 2 to April 1.
West Cumberland	Sept. 15 to March 31	Nov. 14 to March 10.
Wye	...	
Yorkshire . . .	Sept. 1 to Feb. 1	Nov. 16 to last of Feb.

All dates are inclusive.

Use of Gaff

A gaff can only be legally used in the following districts between the dates mentioned ; elsewhere no time is fixed, so it can be used during all the fishing season for rods :—

Coquet	Feb. 1 to Sept. 30.
Conway	May 1 to Oct. 31.
Dart	April 2 to Oct. 15.
Derwent	July 1 to Nov. 14.
Dovey	May 31 to Oct. 20.
Eden	July 1 to Nov. 15.
Exe	March 15 to Sept. 30.
Kent	June 2 to Oct. 31.
Rhymney	May 1 to Nov. 1.
Ribble	May 1 to Nov. 1.
Sciont	March 2 to Nov. 1.
Taff and Ely . . .	June 1 to Nov. 1.
Taw and Torridge . .	June 1 to Nov. 15.
Teign	May 1 to Sept. 1.
Usk	May 1 to Nov. 1.
Wye	March 15 to Nov. 1.
West Cumberland . .	July 1 to Nov. 13.
Yorkshire	May 1 to Nov. 1.

All dates are inclusive.

Use of Nets

In the following districts by-laws defining the kind of nets for salmon, the size of mesh, the use of nets at night, and the use of nets for fish

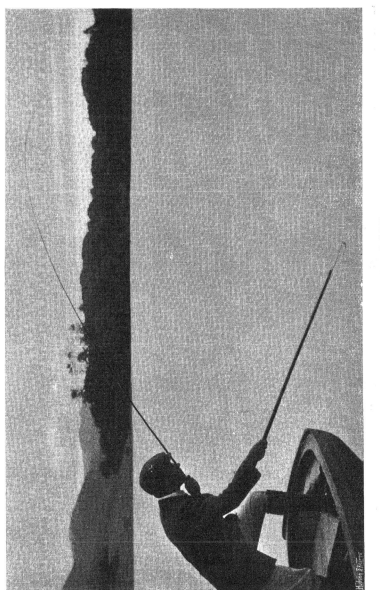

105—USE OF GAFF.

268   A GOOD HAUL ON THE WYE

other than salmon during the close time have been
made :—

District.	Kind of Net.	Mesh of Net.*	Night Netting.	Use of Net for other Fish.
Adur.		+	−	
Avon and Stour .			−	−
Avon (Devon) .		+	−	
Axe	−	−	−	
Ayron	−	−	−	
Camel		−	−	
Cleddy		−	−	−
Coquet	−	−	−	
Cuckmere . . .			−	
Dart	−			−
Dee	−	+	−	−
Dovey		+		
Eden	−	−		
Elwy and Clwyd			−	
Exe			−	−
Fowey	−	−	−	
Kent.			−	
Lune			−	
Ogmore . . .	−	−	−	
Ouse (Sussex) .		+	−	
Rhymney . . .	−	−	−	
Ribble	−			
Rother			−	
Seiont			−	−
Severn	−		−	−
Taff and Ely . .	−		−	
Taw and Torridge	−		−	−
Tamar and Plym	−	−		
Tees	−			−
Teify	−	−		
Teign	−		−	−
Towy	−	−		−
Trent			−	
Tyne		−		
Usk	−	−	−	−
Wye	−	+	−	−
Yorkshire . . .	−		−	

* + means an increase, − a decrease.

The other salmon by-laws relate to weekly close time, fishing at the mouth of rivers with nets, fixing the time when gratings are to be kept up, form of licence, marking and labelling nets and boats.

The rate at which licence duties are payable in the different districts in England and Wales varies greatly. The following table gives every fishery district in England and Wales and the sum charged for rods. Nets vary with the size and nature of the net used :—

District.	Salmon.*					Trout and Char.			
	£	s.	d.			s.	d.		
Eden	1	1	0	season	×	2	6	season	×
Derwent	1	0	0	,,	×	5	0	,,	×
West Cumberland . .	0	10	6	,,	×	2	6	,,	×
Kent	0	10	0	,,	×	5	0	,,	×
Lune	1	0	0	,,	×	2	6	,,	
Ribble	1	0	0	,,	×	5	0	,,	×
Dee	1	0	0	,,	×			...	
Elwy and Clwyd . . .	1	0	0	,,		4	6	,,	×
Conway	1	0	0	,,	×	1	0	,,	×
Seiont	1	1	0	,,	×	5	0	,,	×
Dwyfach	1	1	0	,,	×	7	0	,,	×
Dovey	1	0	0	,,	×	1	0	,,	
Ayron	0	10	0	,,	×	2	6	,,	×
Teifi	1	0	0	,,	×	2	6	,,	
Cleddy	0	10	6	,,		3	6	,,	×
Towy	1	1	0	,,		2	6	,,	
Ogmore	0	10	6	,,		2	0	,,	
Taff and Ely	0	10	6	,,		2	6	,,	
Rhymney	0	10	0	,,		1	0	,,	
Usk and Ebbw . . .	1	0	0	,,		1	0	,,	
Wye	1	0	0	,,	×	1	0	,,	
Severn	0	10	0	,,		2	0	,,	×
Avon, Brue, and Parret .	0	7	6	,,		2	6	,,	×
Taw and Torridge . .	1	4	0	,,				...	

* The cross means that licence for a shorter period or for a smaller area than the whole district can be had at lower rates.

District—*continued.*	Salmon.*				Trout and Char.			
	£	s.	d.		s.	d.		
Camel	o	12	o	season ×	4	o	season	×
Fowey	o	15	o	,,	5	o	,,	
Tamar and Plym . . .	o	7	6	,,			...	
Avon (Devon)	1	o	o	,,	10	o	,,	×
Dart	1	o	o	,, ×	10	o	,,	×
Teign	1	o	o	,, ×	2	6	,,	
Exe	1	o	o	,, ×	2	6	,,	×
Otter			...				...	
Axe	o	10	o	,,	2	6	,,	
Frome	1	o	o	,,			...	
Avon and Stour . . .	1	o	o	,,	5	o	,,	×
Adur	o	5	o	,,	1	o	,,	
Ouse (Sussex)	o	5	o	,,			...	
Cuckmere	o	5	o	,,	1	o	,,	
Rother			...				...	
Stour (Canterbury) . .	1	o	o	,,			...	
Suffolk and Essex . . .			...				...	
Norfolk and Suffolk, E .			...				...	
Norfolk and Suffolk, W .			...				...	
Ouse and Nene . . .			...				...	
Welland			...				...	
Witham			...		2	6	,,	×
Trent	o	10	o	,,	2	6	,,	×
Yorkshire	1	o	o	,,	1	o	,,	
Esk (Yorkshire) . . .	o	10	o	,, ×	1	6	,,	×
Tees	1	o	o	,,	2	6	,,	
Wear	o	5	o	,,	2	o	,,	
Tyne	1	o	o	,, ×	2	6	,,	×
Coquet	o	5	o	,,	2	6	,,	

* The cross means that licence for a shorter period or for a smaller area than the whole district can be had at lower rates.

Where no figures are inserted no licences are issued. The figures are the maximum.

By-laws have also been made as to the annual close time for trout and char in certain districts. When the district is not mentioned, the close time is that fixed by statute—from the 1st October to the 2nd February inclusive. If the instrument is not specified the close time applies to all modes of capture.

District.	Trout.	Char.
Adur	Oct. 1 to March 31	...
Avon (Devon) . .	Oct. 1 to Feb. 28	...
Avon and Stour .	Oct. 1 to March 31	...
Ayron	Oct. 1 to March 15	...
Camel	Oct. 1 to March 15	...
Cleddy	Sept. 29 to March 1	...
Coquet	*Nov. 1 to March 3	...
Cuckmere . . .	Oct. 1 to March 31	...
Dart	Oct. 2 to Feb. 28	...
Dee	*Oct. 14 to Feb. 14	...
Derwent . . .	Sept. 15 to March 10	Nov. 1 to June 30.
Eden	*Oct. 2 to Feb. 28	...
„	†Sept. 2 to Feb. 28	...
Esk (Yorkshire) .	Oct. 1 to March 15	...
Elwy and Clwyd	Oct. 2 to Feb. 28	...
Exe	Sept. 15 to last Feb.	...
Fowey	Oct. 1 to April 30	...
Kent	Oct. 2 to March 3	...
Lune	Oct. 2 to March 1	...
Norfolk & Suffolk	†Sept. 10 to Jan. 25	...
Ouse and Nene .	Oct. 2 to March 31	...
Ribble	Oct. 2 to March 1	...
Seiont	Oct. 2 to March 1	Oct. 22 to March 1.
Severn	Oct. 2 to March 1	...
Suffolk and Essex	Oct. 2 to April 10	...
Taff and Ely . .	Sept. 20 to Feb. 1	...
Tees	Oct. 1 to March 1	...
Teify	Oct. 1 to Feb. 28	...
Teign	Oct. 1 to March 2	...
Towy	Oct. 2 to March 1	...
Trent	Oct. 2 to March 15	...
Tyne	Oct. 1 to March 21	...
Usk and Ebbw .	Oct. 2 to Feb. 14	...
Wear	Oct. 2 to March 1	...
West Cumberland	Sept. 2 to March 10	...
Wye	Oct. 2 to March 1	...
Yorkshire . . .	Oct. 1 to March 15	...

* Rods.   † Nets.

Some districts have made by-laws as to *fresh water* fish. There is no power to vary the close time 15th March to 15th June, fixed by statute, but there is a power given to exempt the whole or part of the district from the close time and to exempt all or certain kinds of fish. The following districts have exercised this power :—

District.	Extent of District Exempted.	Kind of Fish.
Avon (Devon)	Whole	All
Avon and Stour	„	„
Eden	„	„
Kent	„	Pike
Severn	„	„
„	Part	All but Grayling
Towy	Whole	All
Usk	„	Eels
Wye	„	All
Yorkshire	„	Pike
„	Part	All

In all the rest of England and Wales the close time applies to all fresh water fish.

The following districts have made by-laws as to the kind of instrument that may be used for taking fresh water fish and the minimum size of mesh :—

District.	Kind of Instrument.	Size of Mesh.
Adur	—	...
Avon, Brue, and Parret	—	1¾ inch
Avon and Stour		...
Camel	—	...
Cuckmere	—	...
Derwent		1 inch
Exe	—	...
Fowey	—	...
Kent	—	—
Lune	—	...
Ouse and Nene	—	...
Norfolk and Suffolk	—	...
Ribble		2½ inches
Severn	—	1⅜ Bush nets
Suffolk and Essex	—	...
Towy	—	1 inch
Trent	—	...
Usk		1 inch
Wear	—	...
Welland	—	...
Witham	—	...
Wye	—	1 inch

Except in the places mentioned there is no restriction on taking fresh water fish or on the mesh of nets used for that purpose.

The Thames has a series of by-laws of its own, made under the Thames Conservancy Acts. Under these, in the Thames above London Bridge, only a rod and line and certain specified nets can be used, the nets may only be used of the size, in the way, and at the places fixed for their use. Below London Bridge other kinds of nets may be used in the ways mentioned. No trout may be taken between 11th September and 31st March, and no other fish above London Bridge between

15th March and 15th June. No night fishing is allowed. All fishing in certain preserves is prohibited. The Thames has regulations as to the size of fish that may be taken, and as this is not the case elsewhere the sizes are given. The measurements are the extreme length of the fish in inches :—Pike 18, perch 8, chub 10, roach 7, dace 6, barbel 16, trout 16, grayling 12, bream 10, carp 10, tench 8, rudd 6, gudgeon 4, flounder 7, smelts 6, lampeons 7, soles and slips 8, whiting 7, plaice and dabs 8.

Norfolk and Suffolk have also a special code of their own. Conservators are appointed for the rivers in these counties who have all the powers of conservators under the Freshwater Fisheries Acts, and also certain additional powers in making by-laws. They have made by-laws as to close time, the kind of nets to be used, and the mode of using them, the size and mesh of nets, the use of trimmers, and the taking bait and eels.

The Tweed.—This is another place which has its own special Acts. The Tweed Commissioners, the body in whom the management of the Tweed fisheries is vested, have under the Tweed Fisheries Act, 1857, and the Tweed Fisheries Act, 1859, very wide, it might almost be said arbitrary powers, for the prevention of poaching. These powers differ from any power possessed by any other authority in England or Scotland chiefly in being much more severe. But they do not avail to stop poaching, nor, what is perhaps still more needed, to stop the pollution of the river. It should be borne in mind that in the Tweed watershed none of the English or Scotch fishery Acts or by-laws apply.

Scotch Fishery Laws are to a great extent peculiar to Scotland, various fundamental points causing them to differ from the law of England and Ireland. The most important of these are : (1) That all salmon fishing by any means but angling is presumed by Scotch law to belong to the Crown, so that no one can take salmon except with rod and line, unless he can show a royal grant, either express, or implied from long use. It follows from this that no riparian owner in Scotland has, as such, the right to net for salmon in the water adjoining his own lands, whether tidal or non-tidal. He *may* have it, but if so he has it by a title other than that by which he holds his lands. (2) That as salmon seem to have been the only fish the old Scotch law regarded, none of the restrictive legislation applies to other fish than salmon, unless expressly named in the act, so that the riparian owners can take them as they please ; and this right to the fish, by some analogy to the salmon, has been decided by the Scotch Courts to be a right that does not necessarily pass with a lease of lands to a tenant, thus in a lease to an agricultural tenant, which makes no mention of the right of fishing, the right to fish for trout remains with the landlord. (3) That while statute has restricted the capture of salmon in inland waters to net and coble fishing by the Crown grantees, and to angling by the riparian owners,

107.—TWEED—FIFTEEN LARGE SALMON.

108.—TARBERT NET POLES.

and in tidal to fixed engines and net and coble by
the Crown grantees, yet as to all other fish than
salmon, in the case of riparian owners, and those
whose rights are derived from them, the restrictions
do not apply, but only to the general public and
persons who have no right to fish. (4) That by
Scotch law persons cannot be proceeded against summarily for fishing unless they are fishing in some way
prohibited by statute. A trespasser who is angling
can only be proceeded against by action, there being
nothing in the Scotch laws to make a trespasser
fishing in a legal way where he has no right to fish
liable to a penalty on a summary conviction unless
he is guilty of the further offence of using some
method of fishing prohibited by statute. The remedy
for legal fishing is a civil, not a criminal one.

In some respects, therefore, the Scotch law is far
clearer and simpler than the English, and when the
two main principles are understood—that salmon is
a royal fish, and that riparian owners can catch other
fish as they like and when they like, it does not in
ordinary cases present much difficulty. The important questions which arise from time to time,
and which involve very great difficulties, are in
cases where the right to catch salmon is claimed
against the Crown by an individual. Here it is a
case of evidence; the claimant has to prove his case,
and this often gives rise to very great difficulties,
which it is not necessary to consider here. It
should, however, be said that no proof of length
of user of rod fishing is evidence of a grant from

the Crown of salmon fishing, nor is the proof of the use of any kind of net fishing other than some form of net and coble fishing, as all other forms of netting are illegal, and proof of illegal modes will not give rise to an inference of a legal grant.

Another rule of the Scotch law of great practical importance is that to use any new or *unusual* mode of catching fish is illegal. It is not illegal to use net and coble so constantly as practically to intercept all the fish, but to introduce some new mode, such as hang nets, although possibly far less destructive, would be illegal. It is on this principle that the Scotch law prevents the setting up of new fixed engines in tidal and non-tidal waters. But this rule does not exclude the use of improvements in old modes of fishing; this was settled in the celebrated Bermoney boat case, which held that a new mode of working net and coble fisheries, which had been introduced on the Tay, was legal.

The Scotch rule as to access to the river for salmon fishing differs from that in England. This also follows the idea of the salmon being a royal fish, and the right to fish is derived from a royal grant, so that the Crown also gave as an incident the right to the free use of the grant, and therefore access to the river on both banks, as an accessory to the right of salmon fishing other than rod fishing. In England no such right would exist, as the reason for it does not apply to English law. This right does not apply as a rule of law to angling, as that is a

109.—POOL BELOW THE OLD OAK.

110.—THE MINUTES AFTER SUNSET.

right not necessarily derived from the Crown, but from the owners of the land.

Another distinction between the English and Scotch law is that of close time; except as to salmon, there is no close time in Scotland.

The method of administering the law in Scotland differs considerably from England. The Scotch Fishery Board have there control of matters. Every river in Scotland which flows into the sea and its tributaries forms a district, and the Fishery Board fixes the close time for fishing in it. The close time for all modes of fishing but angling must be 168 days; but the Board can fix when they shall begin and end. They also fix the angling close time, but it must not begin earlier nor end later than the other close time. Weekly close time in Scotland has this important difference to England. It is in England and on the Tweed no offence to angle on Sunday; in Scotland it is illegal to angle on the Sabbath.

Each district has a local Board whose chief duties are to carry out the by-laws and orders of the Central Board, and to see to the protection of the river. The mode they raise their funds is quite different from England. A roll of the proprietors of the fisheries in the district is made up on which the value of each fishery is entered, and a rate to raise the necessary sum is levied on the proprietors.

The powers of the Board as to dealing with poachers are in some respect more, and in some less stringent than in England. The differences are mostly very technical, and it would involve too much space to set them out at length. One, however, may be noticed. In England if a person fishes without the express leave of the owner, and obtains it afterwards, no conviction would follow. The Scotch rule is that the express permission must be clearly proved to have been given beforehand, as no subsequent ratification or sanction will do away with the fact of the illegality of the fishing, and a conviction should follow unless it is proved.

As to fish other than salmon, the Scotch law prohibits, under a penalty, a number of modes of taking fish in the main the same as those prohibited in England; but the section goes on to say that the riparian owner and any one authorised by him may in his own fishery exercise the right of fishing in any mode not prohibited by law before the Act of 1860 (23 and 24 Vict. c. 45). It would therefore seem that a riparian owner in Scotland can take fish other than salmon in any way he likes, except it be by weirs or by poisoning the water, these two having been illegal in 1860.

A point that has given rise to much discussion, and cannot be said even yet to be finally settled, is whether clean salmon caught by rod in close time in Scotland can be legally sold in Scotland. The importance of the point is that if the sale in Scotland is legal, the sale in England would also be so. It is rash to give any opinion on so controverted a point; but although justices probably would not, it seems most likely the High Court of Justice would, hold such sale illegal.

In Ireland the fishery law is the same as in England, except so far as it has been altered by statutes applying solely to Ireland. Of these there are a large number ; and the Irish statute law as to fisheries is even more confused than the English, as there are more Acts in force. In the main provisions, however, the English and Irish laws as to salmon are very similar, mainly from the fact that the English Salmon Act of 1861 was a copy more or less slavish of the law then in force in Ireland. Ireland had already been divided into fishery districts with Boards of Conservators. The mode of election differed, the Irish Boards being mainly elected by the licensees, and not nominated by public bodies as in England. Their powers are very similar to those of the English bodies. Their funds are raised by licence duties on the instruments used, as in England, but they are supplemented by rates, which is not the case in England. There is one very important difference in the Irish and English systems. In England a rod licence only avails in the district for which it is taken out, so that a man who goes about fishing requires a number of licences. In Ireland a rod licence, wherever taken out, is available in all parts of Ireland just as a game licence. The rate to raise funds which the Fishery Boards are authorised to levy is such sum as will make up the amount from licences paid by each fishery to a sum equal to 10 per cent. of what the fishery would pay on the poor law valuation in force.

The rules as to fixed engines, bag nets, and weirs are much the same as those in England. No fixed engine that was not in use in 1862, and no bag net not in use in July 1863, can be legally used. All fishing weirs must have free gaps. Taking salmon except with rod and line in mill pools or mill races is made illegal. Night netting—that is, from 8 P.M. to 6 A.M.—for salmon or trout is illegal. A very important provision that does not exist in English law is the prohibition of netting for salmon and trout in all inland waters except by the owner of the fishery. The close season, unless varied, begins on the 15th September, and must last 168 days. But there is power to fix when these 168 days shall begin and end. For angling for salmon and trout the statutory close time is from the 1st March to 1st February. For trout fishing other than angling, from 29th September to the last of February. For eels the close time is 10th January to 1st July. There is not in Ireland any penalty for fishing on Sunday with a rod and line during the open season. In Ireland the weekly close time extends not only to salmon but also to trout. As to dealing with poachers, the Irish law is much the same as the English, the Larceny Act, 1861, applying to Ireland. An Irish Act makes entering on lands for the purpose of, or under pretence of, fishing without the written leave of the owner or occupier an offence, and also resisting or obstructing persons lawfully engaged in fishing, proceeding to fish, or returning from fishing, or placing nets or engines to prevent fish entering the nets of persons set or placed legally. The powers of the English Game Act, 1 and 2 Will. IV. c. 32, sec. 31, as to offenders being obliged to give their names and addresses, and the power of arrest similar to those under the Night Poaching Act, 9 Geo. IV. c. 69, sec. 7, are practically extended to fishing by the Irish Acts.

Although in the main the Irish law is the same as the English, there are considerable differences in points of detail, so it is not safe to assume that what is a breach of the law in one country is a breach in the other. It must also be further borne in mind that there are numerous local alterations by by-laws of the Irish statute law, and it is not safe to assume that the law in any particular place is the law as it appears even in the Irish statutes without an up-to-date inquiry at the office of the Clerk of the Peace of the county where any breach of the law is supposed to have occurred.

APPENDIX.

In this Appendix are given forms of—

(1) An agreement for angling;
(2) An agreement for fishing rights;
(3) A lease of fishing rights for a term.

(1) Agreement for Angling

An Agreement made and entered into this day of   19   , between A   B of   (hereinafter called the lessor), of the one part, and C   D   of   (hereinafter called the tenant), of the other part

If the agreement is on behalf of a Society, it would be well to state it as C   D,   the Secretary of the Angling Society, on behalf of such Society.

Whereby the lessor agrees to let and the tenant agrees to take the [sole] right to angle with rod and line from the lands [of the lessor] adjoining the river   , in the parish of   , in the county of   , and numbered   on the 25-inch Ordnance Survey map for that county, for the term of   , and so on from [year to

If the exclusive right of angling is let, insert the word "sole"; if only a right to fish with others, strike it out. If the agreement is with the tenant, say, "*from the lands in the occupation of the lessor.*" If the lands are on *one* side of the river only, say, "on the left or right bank," as the case may be. If it is desired to limit the angling to any particular kind, this can be done by saying, to angle "with an artificial fly," or "with a single rod and line," if it is desired to restrict the use of two rods. If the term is for less than a year, no provision as to notice will be required. If for a month, it is a calendar month, unless a lunar month is mentioned.

year], until this agreement is terminated in manner hereinafter mentioned, at a rent of   , payable in advance on the execution of these presents, and subject to the provisions hereinafter contained (that is to say).

Unless the landlord gets the right to have the rent paid in advance, he has no security for payment.

The tenant hereby agrees

1. To pay the sum of £   on the execution of these presents [and the further sum of £ on the first of   , as long as the tenancy hereby created continues].

This will be weekly, monthly, half-yearly, or yearly, as the case may be.

2. Not to fish in the said waters in any other way than by [angling with a rod and line with an artificial fly ; not to use any spinning bait, natural or artificial].

Here insert any restrictions on the mode of fishing.

3. Not to use any net, gaff, or instrument (except a landing-net), other than a rod and line, for taking fish.

This should be altered to meet the special case.

4. Not to retain any fish of a less size than inches in extreme length. And if any of a less length be caught, at once to return them to the water with the least possible injury.

If for salmon, this should be weight rather than size. For an idea of size, see Thames By-laws.

5. Not to take or retain if taken, any unclean or unseasonable fish, but at once to return it to the water with the least possible injury.

6. Not to take or attempt to take more than   fish in any one day.

This is very stringent, but is necessary on some waters, especially if efforts are being made to get up a stock of fish.

7. Not to do any unnecessary damage to the fences, fields, and crops on the lands adjoining the river over which the tenant may pass, and to make good or compensate the person who may have sustained any such damage.

This may be extended to disturbing game, bringing dogs, or any other thing it is desired to prevent.

8. To quit and deliver up the fishery at the expiration of   [calendar month], on notice in writing signed by the lessor or his agent, and either personally delivered to or sent by post to the tenant's last known address.

Fill in the blank with week, month, or as the case may be.

The lessor hereby agrees—

9. Not during the currency of this agreement to allow more than   persons to fish in the said waters.

Unless some restriction is placed, the landlord could grant as many rights to angle as he pleased. This will not apply if the *sole* right is let.

10. Not to net or permit any netting to be carried on in the said waters.

It might be well to alter this, so as to keep down coarse fish.

11. Not to fish himself or allow any other person to fish with any device or mode of fishing other than is allowed to the tenant.

12. To prosecute or allow the tenant to use his name in prosecuting all persons who may be found illegally or unlawfully fishing in the said waters.

13. To efficiently protect the said waters from all illegal or unlawful fishing.

14. To have any weeds, boughs, or bushes, which interfere with the fishing, cut at the tenant's request and kept cut [at the tenant's expense].

15. To take all steps that may be necessary to secure to the tenant uninterrupted access to the said waters at all times during the continuance of this agreement.

16. Not to do or permit to be done any act or thing that shall interfere with the due exercise by the tenant of his rights to fish as granted by this agreement.

17. That the tenant paying the rent, and performing the stipulations herein on his part contained, shall quietly enjoy the right to fish as granted by this agreement during the continuance thereof, and the lessor hereby authorises the tenant on his behalf to exercise all powers and rights of seizure of tackle given to the lessor by the Larceny Law Consolidation Act, 1886, or any other statutes.

In witness, &c.,   (L. S.)

The stipulations on the part of the lessor are those that would usually be required for the tenant's protection. It must be remembered that a grant of leave to angle does not impose any obligation on the grantor except to allow the tenant to angle, and the tenant must therefore protect himself. The lessor could, after granting the licence, net or let others net, or allow any number of persons to fish in any way they like. The tenant has no right to prosecute. The lessor is not bound to protect the tenant, even to get weeds and bushes cut. Hurdles or barbed wire may be placed along the banks of the river. Gravel may be carted out, or a drain made into the river. Other special clauses may be required to meet certain cases, but most of the above will be wanted in all lettings.

Two things must be borne in mind. (1) To ascertain if the lessor has the right to grant the permission to fish. If the landlord is the grantor, then unless the land is in hand, it must be seen that the fishing is reserved in the lease or agreement. If the tenant grants the permission, it must be seen that the fishing is *not* reserved to the landlord. (2) That the agreement must be under seal, otherwise it is useless, and gives the tenant no legal rights.

(2) AGREEMENT FOR LETTING FISHING RIGHTS.

An Agreement made and entered into the   day of   19 ,   , between A   B   of (hereinafter called the lessor), of the one part, and C   D   of   [or C   D   , E   F   , and G   H   , members of and on behalf of the Society] (hereinafter called the tenants), of the other part.

Whereby the lessor agrees to let, and the tenants to take, all the lessor's rights of fishing in the river [or pool, or lake as the case may be], in the parish of   , in the county of   , in or adjoining the lands of the lessor in the occupation of   [or in his own occupation], known as [set out names]. [The description, by reference to the Ordnance map, is best, but this is given as an alternative form], for the term of [set out week, month, or year] from the   day of   , at the rent of £   per [week, or month, or year], the first rent to be paid on the execution of these presents, and the subsequent rent in advance on the first day of each successive [week, month, or year], during which the tenancy continues, upon the terms and conditions hereinafter contained.

The tenants agree with the lessor—

1. To pay the rent at the times hereinbefore appointed for payment, and to pay any rates, taxes, and assessments that may become payable, other than land tax, landlords' property tax, and tithe rent charge.

2. To keep up and maintain a good stock of fish, and not to allow the stock to decrease below its present condition.

3. Not to use any unlawful means or modes of fishing, or any means or modes of fishing that are, or may be, unduly destructive.

4. To preserve the fish in the said fishery, and to prosecute all poachers and persons who shall illegally fish in the fishery.

5. Not to allow any unclean or unseasonable fish to be taken.

6. Not to use any net in the said fishery within *one month* of the termination of this agreement.

The lessor agrees with the tenants—

7. Not to do, or permit to be done, any act that will injure or damage the fishery.

8. To keep and maintain free access to the fishery, and all parts thereof for the tenants, their agents, and servants.

9. To prosecute, or allow the tenants to use his name in prosecuting, all persons found poaching or illegally fishing, and to authorise the tenants, or their servants, to exercise on his behalf all powers of seizure given by the Larceny Act, 1866, or by any other statutes.

10. That the tenants paying the rent and performing the agreements and conditions above contained shall quietly enjoy the said fishery during the continuance of this agreement.

In witness, &c.

(L. S.)

This agreement is in the simplest form possible. All the necessary special clauses to meet any case can be taken either from the preceding or succeeding forms, and altered to suit the particular case. Much depends on the kind of fishing and what is wanted to be done. No. 6 has been inserted to prevent a tenant taking out the best fish before leaving.

This must be under *seal*, and all that has been said as to the right of the lessor to enter into the agreement under No. 1 applies equally here. Any agreement for a house or shooting, or any other take, can easily be adapted for fishing by adding the appropriate clauses and executing it under seal.

(3) LEASE OF FISHING RIGHTS

This Indenture, made this   day of   , 19 , between A   B   , of   (hereinafter called the lessor), of the one part, and C   D   , of   [or E   F   , G   H   , &c., of   , members of, and on behalf of, the   Fishery Society], (hereinafter called the lessee), of the other part. *Whereas* the lessor is entitled to the exclusive right of fishing in that part of the river   [or as may be], in the parish of   , in the county of   , as adjoins the lands of the lessor, in the occupation of   , as tenant of the lessor [or in the occupation of the lessor as tenant for a term of   years created by an indenture of lease, dated the   day of   , 19 , and expressed to be made between (parties), or as the case may be], and which lands are numbered respectively   , on the Ordnance Survey map of the said parish, on the scale of 25 inches to a mile, and has agreed to demise all his said right of fishing to the lessee for the term at the rent, and subject to the covenants and conditions hereinafter contained. *Now this Indenture witnesseth*, that in pursuance of the said agreement, and in consideration of the rent hereby reserved, and the covenants and conditions herein contained, he, the lessor, does hereby let unto the lessee, his executors, administrators, and assigns, *All that*, the lessor's exclusive right of fishing in the river   , in the parish of   , in the county of   , where it adjoins the lands of the lessor in the said parish, and which said lands are numbered respectively [fill in numbers] on the Ordnance Survey map of the said parish, drawn on the scale of 25 inches to the mile, and are now in the occupation of [fill in name], as tenant to the lessor : *To hold* the said fishery for the term of   years from the day of next, yielding and paying in advance the annual rent of   by equal half-yearly payments on the   day of   and the   day of in each year, the first of such payments to be made on the   day of   next. And the lessee for himself, his heirs, executors, and administrators, covenants with the lessor, his heirs, and assigns [or his executors, administrators, and assigns as the case may be] that he will pay the rent hereby reserved on the days hereinbefore appointed for payment, and will pay and discharge all rates, taxes, and assessments whatever that shall during the continuance of these presents be levied or made upon the said fishery, landlord's property tax, land tax, and tithe rent charge (if any) only excepted : *And will* protect and

preserve the said fishery from all illegal fishing,
poaching, trespassing, and will proceed against and
prosecute any person who may be found poaching,
trespassing, or illegally fishing in the said fishery,
and will not permit or suffer any person or persons
to do any act or thing contrary to the right and
title of the lessor to the said fishery, and will use
his best endeavour to keep down all pike, coarse
fish, and all other fish that may be likely to interfere
with the proper development and maintenance of
the fishery as a trout fishery, and will not allow any
trout or grayling to be taken out of season or in an
unclean state, or of a size less than   inches [or
under a certain length], and will not allow any trout
or grayling to be taken otherwise than by rod and
line [or by artificial fly], and will not take, or permit to be taken in any one day, more than
trout and   grayling, and will not take, or
allow to be taken, from any fish caught in the said
fishery any ova except for the purpose of artificial
hatching for stocking the said fishery, and will not
sell, part with, or in any way dispose of other than
by turning the same into the said fishery any fry,
yearlings, or other fish that may have been bred
in any hatchery or other place for the artificial
propagation of fish connected with the said
fishery : *And will* not turn down, or permit to
be turned down, or put into the said fishery,
any fish, whether British or imported from
abroad, except the different species of the genus
salmon, without the previous written consent of the

lessor or his authorised agent : *And will* in each year turn into the said fishery not less than
healthy yearling trout, either produced or bred in the hatcheries connected with the fishery, or bred elsewhere in the United Kingdom, and produce to the lessor or his agent satisfactory evidence of the place of purchase, number and condition of the trout so turned down, and in default will pay to the lessor such sum not exceeding £   by way of additional rent as will enable the lessor to obtain in the next season a number of healthy yearling trout sufficient to make up the annual number : *And will* at least
      times a year net out and destroy all pike and coarse fish there may be in the said fishery, and will every year furnish to the lessor a return of all the pike and coarse fish netted out and killed. *Provided always*, and these presents are upon the express condition, that if the rent hereby reserved shall be in arrears for twenty-one days after the days herein fixed for payment, whether the same shall have been legally demanded or not, or if the lessee shall commit any breach of any of the covenants, agreements, and conditions on his part to be performed herein contained, that then the lessor may at any time thereafter re-enter upon the same premises, and the term hereby created shall thereupon cease and determine, but without prejudice to the right of the lessor to recover all rent due and damages for any covenant and condition which the lessee has broken. *And the lessor* does hereby, for himself, his heirs, executors, and administrators covenant with the

lessee, his executors, and administrators that he will
at all times during the continuance of the term
hereby created, use his best endeavour that the
supply of water to the said fishery should be maintained both in quantity and quality in as good a
condition as it was at the date of these presents, and
will prevent by all reasonable means any pollution
of the water of the said fishery so as to be
prejudicial thereto, and will not do anything by
himself or his agents, or permit anything to be
done which will interfere with the free passage of
trout or grayling to or from the said fishery, or
that will change or alter the nature and condition
of the river or its bed at the said fishery, and will
at the written request of the lessee cut down and
remove such bushes, trees, and shrubs growing on
the banks of the said river adjoining the said fishery
as may be prejudicial thereto, and will plant such
trees, shrubs, and bushes as may be reasonably
required for shelter or otherwise for the benefit of
the said fishery, and will not by himself or servants
take, or agree to take, nor permit his tenants or
workmen, to take gravel, sand, or material from the
bed of the river in the said fishery which shall
damage or injure the same, nor suffer any fenc-
ing, planting, or other work to be done that will
interfere with the free access of the lessee, his
servants and agents, to the fishery: And that the
lessee, paying the rent and performing the covenants herein contained, shall quietly possess and
enjoy the said fishery during the continuance of

these presents : And will at all time during the
continuance of these presents, on the request in
writing of the tenant authorise such persons as
the tenant may nominate to exercise all rights of
seizure of tackle or nets given to the lessor by
the Larceny Law Consolidation Act, 1866, or any
other statutes : Provided always, and it is hereby
agreed between the parties hereto, that if either of
them is desirous of determining the term hereby
created after the   day of   , that on the
party so desirous giving to the other
calendar months' notice in writing before the
day of   in any year of his intention to
determine the same that then, on the expiration of
such notice, the term hereby created shall, as on the
         day of   next after the receipt of
such notice, cease and determine : Provided also
that if the lessee is desirous of assigning or parting
with the possession of the term hereby created to a
satisfactory, qualified, responsible person, of which
the lessor shall be sole judge, the lessee shall be at
liberty to assign the residue of the said term to such
person if the assent in writing of the lessor or his
agent has been previously obtained.

In witness, &c.

This lease must be under seal. In most cases it
will be found too stringent, but it was considered as
well to insert all the clauses required, as they can
readily be omitted. If the lease is of a coarse fish
fishery, considerable modification will be wanted.

The idea has been to try and provide (1) all proper restrictions on the lessee's fishing, (2) provisions for keeping up the stock of fish, (3) provisions for preventing the fishery being turned into a fish farm, and from having objectionable fish introduced ; while to protect the tenant the landlord has been made to covenant as to the water supply both for quantity and quality, to keep the river as near as possible in the same state, and not to allow his tenants to injure the fishery. Here again it will require modification in each case, but the important special points from a fishing point of view are, it is believed, inserted. All the precautions as to the rights of the lessor to grant it, mentioned above under agreement No. 1, are equally requisite and important here. Careful inquiry should be made from the tenants of the land, not only as to what rights they have been in the habit of exercising, but also as to what rights they claim to exercise.